AURA GARDEN GUIDES

Ilse Höger-Orthner

Container Gardening

AURA BOOKS

Aura Garden Guides

Container Gardens

Ilse Höger-Orthner

Original German language edition:
Gärten leicht und richtig
Kübelpflanzen
© 1995 BLV Verlagsgesellschaft
mbH, München, Germany

This edition produced by:
Transedition Limited for
Aura Books, Bicester
and first published in 2002

English language edition
© 1995 Advanced Marketing (UK) Ltd.,
Bicester, England

English language translation by:
Andrew Shackleton for Translate-A-Book,
a division of Transedition Ltd.,
Oxford

Typesetting by:
Organ Graphic, Abingdon

10 9 8 7 6 5 4 3 2 1
Printed in Dubai

ISBN 1 901683 49 4

CONTENTS

Before we start ...

The urge to create a garden paradise is as old as human thought itself. The legend of the Garden of Eden is an expression of zest for living, and we can visualise it as a riot of flowers.

Across all cultures and continents, gardeners have striven to reach this goal, but the vagaries of climate and weather have set limits to human endeavour. There were many plants which people couldn't grow out in the garden, so what could be more obvious than to grow all those much-coveted exotic plants in tubs and pots?

Nowadays we may consider ourselves more sober and rational, but the motives that inspire us to grow plants in containers are the same as they have ever been.

Gardeners normally distinguish between annuals, container plants and garden plants, but these groupings shouldn't be regarded as botanical divisions. In this book, for reasons of space, we have confined ourselves to the classic container plants, plus a few garden plants that are suitable for containers.

Classic container plants

A number of the huge range of container plants on offer come originally from the tropics and subtropics. However, the majority are from temperate countries. In contrast to annuals, which are exhausted after only a short lifespan, the classic container plants consist mainly of trees, shrubs and large herbaceous perennials or other non-woody plants. These plants differ enormously in the treatment they require, which depends to a large extent on the climate of their native countries.

In their natural habitat, plants have so evolved that they have become naturally suited the ambient conditions. Plants from tropical forests, where light is scarce but moisture is plenty, are noticeably different from those that come from tropical mountain ranges or from the dry regions of the earth. Desert plants will have needed to adapt to dry winds and large fluctuations in temperature, while maritime plants will have been influenced by the proximity of the sea.

Tropical plants, with their large, soft, lush-green leaves, have great trouble surviving in the warm, dry conditions in most homes. Conversely, plants from dry areas have difficulty coping with dark, damp situations. So the successful cultivation of these exotics depends to a large extent on how well you are able to meet their natural requirements.

Tropical plants are accustomed to experiencing only minor fluctuations in temperature, so the best place to grow them is in a heated greenhouse; the conditions here come closest to matching those to be found in their natural habitat. On the other hand, plants from tropical mountain ranges, from deserts, and from areas such as the Mediterranean that are dry in the summer, are all well suited to cultivation as container plants.

Garden plants

Some ordinary garden shrubs are also suitable for cultivation in tubs and containers, provided these meet the necessary conditions for growth. Similarly, dwarf varieties of our many garden trees, or plants that have particular soil requirements, can make good container plants if they receive the appropriate care that they require.

A quiet corner filled with lots of container plants — fuchsias, petunias and sedums, to name but a few

Container plants in history

Building conservatories and surrounding ourselves with container plants isn't just a modern trend. The practice of cultivating plants in containers, or in climatically controlled environments, can be traced back to the earliest of human civilisations.

The Romans adopted greenhouse cultivation from the Greeks. Exotic shrubs and trees were installed in large terracotta tubs and wooden boxes, and during the colder months they were moved into greenhouses. The remains of these have been found in Pompeii. Unfortunately, the Romans' gardening skills disappeared with the collapse of their great empire.

It was several centuries before Mediterranean plants were introduced to other parts of Europe. One of the first of these was rosemary, which is mentioned as early as 794 in Charlemagne's *capitulare de villis* — his pronouncements on country estates. Rosemary was also planted in the monastery garden at St Gallen in Switzerland.

Rosemary was later followed by the citrus fruits, which in ancient times had been highly esteemed as ornamental plants, particularly by the Romans. North of the Alps, citrus fruits were first mentioned in the writings of Hildegard of Bingen and Albertus Magnus in the 12th and 13th centuries. The first lemons were raised in northern Europe as early as about 1550, reaching Britain in the mid-17th century. Well before that time, however, plants from more temperate regions, including native species, were being grown as potted specimens.

From the Age of Discovery onwards, the cultivation of container plants became an established custom throughout Europe.

It wasn't just spices that came to us along the many trading roots that criss-crossed the globe. Many exotic plants found their way into the palaces of the European princes, or into the beautifully kept gardens of the landowning classes.

Tropical plants are flourishing in this lavishly laid-out conservatory.

As early as the 16th century, orange trees were being grown as container plants in gardens of the northern European nobility. Soon no garden was considered complete without its orange and lemon bushes. In summer these plants were used as decoration in front of buildings or along pathways. Then they were overwintered in special wooden sheds. As garden cultivation developed, so the fashion grew for many new and exotic plants, and these simple sheds became increasingly lavish in form. Buildings that had previously served only as temporary winter quarters were transformed into the edifices that we would now call orangeries. These orangeries reached their peak in the

baroque period. Perhaps one of the best examples is to be found at Versailles. Some were as big as palaces, and their function as homes for plants soon became little more than purely symbolic.

Tastes began to change with the Industrial Revolution, and tropical plants became increasingly fashionable. These demanded quarters that better fulfilled their need for more light and heat.

Orangeries had originally just been used for overwintering orange and lemon plants. In the 19th century, however, the term came to be applied to glasshouses in which tropical plants were kept permanently. These giant structures reached their architectural peak in the middle of the last century. The largest and most beautiful — constructed of iron and glass — were built in the grounds of the great European palaces of Karlsruhe, Stuttgart, Munich and Vienna.

These served as a model for the newly prosperous middle classes. As well as large greenhouses, small conservatories were built adjoining houses in the cities. As these were directly attached to the house, they could also serve as an extension of the living space.

The age of vast glasshouses came to an end with the dying echoes of the 19th century. However, modest greenhouses and conservatories have continued to be used right down to the present day. Nowadays they are if anything more popular than ever.

Varied natural conditions

Many gardeners have a dream of raising exotic plants from southern Europe and the Mediterranean. Today, thanks to modern technical aids, such a dream is no longer beyond the scope of most gardeners. This is true even in the colder parts of this country, where conservatories, solaria or lean-to greenhouses can provide excellent winter quarters for these sunloving plants.

It is worth remembering, however, that confined space alone often exposes these plants to very different conditions from those to be found in their native environment. It is therefore perhaps not surprising that some of them have problems surviving in our greenhouses and conservatories.

You should also bear in mind that not everything that looks exotic is suited to one and the same climate. Container plants come from many different climatic zones, and even within these zones there are very marked regional differences. Some plants have evolved on exposed mountainsides, whereas others have always been sheltered from the wind. Others again have grown up next to rivers or lakes, or are used to being very close to the sea.

All these factors are significant. Every plant throughout the world has adapted to the natural conditions of its environment, and its characteristics have been modified accordingly. Thus plants from the dry zones mostly have small, hard, grey or silvery leaves to reduce transpiration to a minimum. Without such an adaptation they would quickly dry out. By contrast, plants from the warm, humid zones of the subtropics and tropics are equipped with large, soft leaves of a lush-green colour. High humidity means they can regulate their temperature through transpiration without any risk of drying out.

These are by no means the only criteria which are significant for the life of plants. Some regions, for example, experience large variations in temperature between day and night, and between the seasons of the year. Other areas, by contrast, enjoy much more uniform conditions.

However, to go into every detail of each particular climatic zone would take up far too much space. Suffice it to say that each plant requires slightly different conditions.

If you want to grow container plants successfully, you need to have a good knowledge of their individual requirements. Only if you fulfil their demands — at least to a certain degree — can you expect to enjoy them for the length of their natural life.

This section, like all the others in this book, includes plants from more than one climatic zone. So, apart from the general advice given at the beginning of each chapter, you should take particular note of the details given on each plant.

This citrus plant is just the right thing for creating a really Mediterranean atmosphere.

Mediterranean plants

This category covers not only plants from the Mediterranean region, but also those from other areas with a similar climate.

If you've ever spent a summer holiday in the Mediterranean, then you'll know the kinds of conditions that prevail there at that time of year. The sun shines relentlessly from early morning onwards, and midday temperatures may often exceed 100°F (38°C). Most of the rainfall occurs in winter months; the summer months by contrast are completely dry.

The plants that live there must be able to retain their water reserves during the hot season. So the leaves of these mostly evergreen plants tend to be small and very leathery or hairy so that very little moisture is lost from them by transpiration. Another common feature is the strong aroma that often emanates from the foliage; the oils that produce this are yet another adaptation to drought. In their natural habitat you can often smell these plants from a long distance away.

Container plants from Mediterranean-type areas demand both adequate feeding and watering, and somewhere frost-free to spend the winter — ideally a cool greenhouse.

 Put Mediterranean plants in as sunny a position as possible. Give them really good drainage, and avoid using plastic containers because of the risk of waterlogging. Give them hard water if possible. Don't move them indoors too early — give them time to harden off. Then overwinter them in very cool but well-lit conditions, only moderately moist.

9

The leaves and berries of the spotted laurel

Spotted laurel
Aucuba japonica
You often see this plant in foyers or entrance halls. As a container plant it is both decorative and extremely robust. Strictly speaking, the spotted laurel is a native of Japan, but as with so many oriental trees and shrubs, you can hardly imagine a Mediterranean garden without it.

Spotted laurels are evergreen. They can be recognised from their leathery, widely toothed, yellow-spotted leaves, and from the large red berries that appear on the female plants. Aucubas are dioecious, which means you need one plant of each sex to produce the attractive berries.

The exceptions are *A. j.* 'Crotonifolia' and the green-leaved *A. j.* 'Rozannie', which are monoecious, having male and female flowers on the same plant.

Flowering: Spring.

Situation: Sunny to shady.

Growing medium: Any really free-draining soil.

Watering/feeding: Water freely when in full growth, and feed moderately once a week.

Overwintering: Hardy to about 5°F (–15°C), but less hardy if the container is allowed to freeze; water only sparingly.

Pests/diseases: Scale insects; black blotches on leaves if overwintered too wet.

Special notes: Tolerates pruning. The berries are poisonous!

Cultivars: Various cultivars with gold-flecked or variegated foliage.

Marguerite
Argyranthemum frutescens
A Mediterranean-style patio can never be properly complete without white or yellow marguerites. These plants always make a beautiful sight, whether grown in a clump or trained as standards.

A. frutescens is in fact a native of the Canary Islands, where it grows to form sizeable shrubs, both on mountain slopes and along the coasts. In its native habitat, this species blooms nearly all year round with only a brief lull.

Flowering: May–September.

Situation: Full sun.

Growing medium: Loamy or humus-rich, chalky and free-draining.

Watering/feeding: Water and feed freely when in full growth.

Routine care: Deadhead and remove dried leaves.

Overwintering: Frost-free, very cool and light. If overwintering in the dark, keep dry and perhaps cut back by a third.

Pests/diseases: Aphids, fungal root infections.

Cultivars: White-flowering with grey-green foliage, or yellow-flowering with green, rather less feathery leaves.

Everyone knows the marguerite (Argyranthemum frutescens).

Rock rose
Cistus

Rock roses are among the most beautiful of all flowering shrubs. They occur throughout the Mediterranean area, and have been known in Britain since about 1650. The leaves exude a sticky, aromatic gum resin that is known as ladanum or labdanum. At one time this was used in medicines a lot, and was also very important in the perfume industry.

Flowering: May–July.

Situation: Full sun, or they won't flower.

Growing medium: Humus-rich, free-draining.

Watering/feeding: During the growing season, water and feed freely.

The rock rose likes a really sunny spot, where its leaves give off a spicy fragrance.

Routine care: Cut back after flowering to keep the plant bushy.

Overwintering: Most plants will tolerate a little frost, but are better overwintered cool, light and fairly dry.

Pests/diseases: Aphids; grey mould (*Botrytis*) in poorly ventilated winter quarters.

Special notes: Petals very fine like tissue paper; free-flowering, but each individual bloom lasts only a few hours; new flowers always opening.

Species/cultivars: *C. laurifolius*, white flowers with yellow centres, extremely hardy; *C. ladanifer*, white flowers with browny-red blotches; *C. × purpureus*, flowers a deep purplish-pink.

Citrus plants

If you want to recreate a Mediterranean-style patio, then you can't do without oranges and lemons.

Maybe your home-grown oranges won't taste quite as good as the supermarket ones, but they're still worth growing, if only because the blossoms have such a gorgeous fragrance. Besides, who could resist the idea of adding a slice of home-grown lemon to their glass of gin and tonic?

To us oranges and lemons are the classic Mediterranean plants. However, most of them come from the warmer parts of western Asia, from where they made their way via Persia to Greece, later spreading rapidly across the whole Mediterranean area.

Citrus plants were initially used mainly for religious or medicinal purposes. But people soon found out how good the fruits tasted, and started to grow and develop them for eating and drinking alone.

Citrus plants soon came into vogue as ornamental plants — particularly in Italy, where Roman villas were decorated with large tubs planted with orange and lemon trees.

People soon discovered how frost-sensitive they were, and that winter protection was needed in colder, more northerly regions. Even in northern Italy, for example, they had to be planted against a south-facing wall, and furnished with wooden structures in winter to protect them against the cold. These lemon houses can still be seen today on the shores of Lake Garda.

Because of our cool climate, oranges were not introduced into Britain until about the middle of the 16th century, and lemons a whole century later. Even then they were grown mainly for the decorative value of their flowers and fruit, rather than for the use of their fruit.

All plants belonging to the genus *Citrus* are evergreen trees or shrubs with large, leathery green leaves and small white flowers possessing a very strong scent. Some of them also have spiny branches. There are too many species and varieties to describe all of them here. So we have confined ourselves to the most important ones, along with those most suitable for growing as container plants.

Citrus-type plants come in a huge variety of forms — here an orange and a kumquat.

Sour, bitter or Seville orange
Citrus aurantium aurantium

The Seville orange forms tall trees with spiny branches and large leaves. The flowers are white and relatively large, and give off an intense fragrance. One characteristic of this subspecies is the broad-winged leaf stalk. The bitter fruits are used to make our world-famous orange marmalade, and Neroli oil is distilled from the flowers.

The species, *C. aurantium*, is also extremely important as one of the two main rootstocks used for grafting (see page 15).

The most interesting variety for use as a container plant is the dwarf form *C. a.* var. *myrtifolia*, better known as the cultivar *C. a.* 'Chinotto'. The chinotto is a low-growing bush with small leaves, dense foliage and a rich display of flowers. The flowers are as large as those of the species, and have a very intense fragrance. The chinotto bears edible fruits, which are used in the preparation of drinks.

Another interesting subspecies is the bergamot (*C. a. bergamia*) with its aromatic foliage and sweetly scented flowers. Its fruits are not usually eaten, however.

Lemon
Citrus limon

Lemon trees are of medium height, with spiny branches and large light-green leaves. The flower buds are reddish, opening into beautifully fragrant

white blooms. *C. limon* is the only citrus species that can bear both flowers and fruits at the same time.

Lemons are especially frost-sensitive because they enter their dormant period later than do other citrus plants. *C. limon* will grow well in a pot, even developing into a proper tree.

There are a large number of good cultivars of *C. limon*. The hardiest is *C. l.* 'Meyerii', which has a thin skin. The fruits of *C. l.* 'Ponderosa' have a rough skin and turn yellowy-orange.

The lemon tree is unusual in being able to blossom and fruit at the same time.

The lemandarin is a cross between a lemon and a mandarin (*C. reticulata*; see overleaf). It also has the advantage of being a very hardy plant.

Pomelo or shaddock
Citrus maxima

This species grows into a very tall, spherical tree. The large, yellowy-orange fruit is known as the pomelo or shaddock.

Citron
Citrus medica
The citron has been cultivated in Europe for longer than any other citrus species, although nowadays it is only grown commercially on Corsica and in parts of southern Italy. It forms large trees or shrubs bearing fragrant white flowers. The fruits have a very thick, rough skin, and are used in the preparation of candied peel.

This orange tree is simply bursting with fruit.

Grapefruit
Citrus × paradisi
The grapefruit probably resulted from a cross between the sweet orange (*C. sinensis*) and the pomelo (*C. maxima*; see previous page). The plant needs a lot of light and sun. The most robust cultivar is *C. × p.* 'Duncan'; *C. × p.* 'Ruby' has pinkish-red flesh.

Mandarin
Citrus reticulata
Mandarins are natives of eastern Asia. They form large shrubs or small trees with spiny branches, dark-green foliage and lots of flowers. The best-known cultivars are tangerines and satsumas. The satsuma group are the most robust, and *C. r.* 'Owari Satsuma' is particularly prolific.

Sweet orange
Citrus sinensis
Sweet oranges are from warmer parts of western Asia, and probably came to Europe with the voyages of discovery. They are the most commonly grown citrus plant, just as oranges are the most commonly eaten fruit.

C. sinensis forms tall trees with dark-green foliage and lots of wonderfully fragrant white flowers in the spring. The fruits ripen between October and April, depending on the cultivar.

The best-known cultivars are 'Moro' and 'Sanguinella' (both early blood oranges), 'Washington' (a medium-early cultivar), 'Tarocco' and 'Valencia Late' (both late cultivars). Any one of these can normally be obtained as a container plant from a good specialist supplier. But the so-called 'orange trees' sold as container plants elsewhere are mostly dwarf forms or hybrids of other citrus species.

Hardy citrus plants
Citrus, Fortunella etc
Constant efforts are made to breed frost-hardy citrus plants. Good results have been achieved by selection and by crossing various species with each other. The plants that have been bred are also very suitable for growing in containers, as

they are not only very hardy but produce delicious fruits. *Citrus* 'Curafora' has fruits the size of peaches. *C.* 'Venasca' grows into a larger plant, with fruits nearly as big as grapefruits.

Often included among the citrus plants are the closely related kumquats (*Fortunella*) from China and Japan. The best-known species are the round kumquat (*F. japonica*) and the oval kumquat (*F. margarita*). Kumquats are noticeably hardier than *Citrus* species: in favoured locations they can stand temperatures as low as 14°F (-10°C). But they need a temperature of at least 68°F (20°C) in order to flower. The flowers are small, while the fruits have a spicy-sweet flavour and can be eaten complete with their skins. One of the best-tasting cultivars is 'Meiwa', with largish round fruits; another good cultivar is 'Nagami', with oval fruits.

Hardier fruit trees have also been produced by hybridising *Citrus* species with kumquats (*Fortunella*) or with the equally hardy Japanese bitter orange (*Poncirus trifoliata*). The best-known *Citrus–Poncirus* hybrid is the citrange (×*Citroncirus webberi*). The limequat (×*Citrofortunella swinglei*) and the calamondin (×*Citrofortunella microcarpa*) are *Citrus–Fortunella* crosses. Both are low-growing plants that flower and fruit while still young, but their fruits are very sour and unpalatable. Calamondins are often confused with kumquats, and are frequently sold as such.

The Seville orange has a very distinctive leaf.

Also of interest is *Microcitrus australasica* — a wild species from Australia that can also be grown as a bonsai.

Before you make your final decision about buying a citrus plant, it is worth noting which of the two common rootstocks has been used for grafting — *Citrus aurantium* (see page 13) or the hardier *Poncirus trifoliata* (Japanese bitter orange; see opposite). Species grafted onto *P. trifoliata* are more frost-tolerant by about 3-7F° (2-4C°). *P. trifoliata* also forms a less vigorous rootstock than the stronger-growing *C. aurantium*. If possible, try to buy a plant with a *less* vigorous rootstock. It will be healthier and more prolific in the long term than a vigorous plant that has been forcibly confined to a pot. The more vigorous plant flowers and fruits more quickly, but the fruit harvest is poor later on.

Flowering: Spring.

Situation: Sunny, bright, sheltered from wind.

Growing medium: Loamy, rich in humus and nutrients, free-draining and slightly acid.

Watering/feeding: Use soft water. Water moderately when in full growth, but don't let the root ball dry out. Keep the soil well drained and avoid water-logging. Give a nitrogen-rich liquid feed once a week until the end of July.

Routine care: Citrus plants will tolerate pruning, and can be trained into various shapes such as a fan or a hollow crown.

Overwintering: Citrus plants vary enormously in their frost tolerance (see above). Lemons and grapefruit can cope with only a slight frost, while oranges and mandarins will tolerate a moderate frost, and a kumquat planted out in the garden can survive temperatures as low as 14°F (-10°C). Overwinter your citrus plants in a light, airy position, keeping them virtually dry; overwatering in winter is fatal. Don't put your plants outside again until all danger of frost is past.

Pests/diseases: Aphids, red spider mites, scale insects; chlorosis if the soil is too chalky or too wet; fungal diseases if the winter quarters are poorly ventilated.

Special notes: The root collar must be clear of the soil. Use large, wide containers.

Lavender
Lavandula

Lavender is found throughout the Mediterranean region, and is also cultivated in this country. The lavender fields of East Anglia are worth a visit in June, when they are in flower and give off the most marvellous fragrance.

Lavender is a medicinal plant, whose disinfectant and antiseptic properties have been known from time immemorial. Extracts are still used for their calming and stimulating effect. But these days lavender is most extensively used in the cosmetic industry. The essential oil from the lavender flower is an important raw material in the preparation of soaps and perfumes.

Lavender is a subshrub with narrow grey-green leaves and spikes of flowers in various shades of blue, depending on the species and cultivar.

Flowering: June–July.

Situation: Full sun.

Growing medium: Humus-rich, free-draining, chalky.

Watering/feeding: Water only moderately; never feed.

Routine care: Cut back after flowering, but take care, because it reacts badly if old wood is cut back too hard.

Overwintering: *L. angustifolia* and *L. stoechas* are hardy, but the other species must be overwintered somewhere frost-free and light, such as in a cool greenhouse.

Pests/diseases: None.

Special notes: If you intend to dry a bunch of flowers, then you should cut them before they're fully open.

Species/cultivars: *L. angustifolia* (old English lavender), also listed as *L. officinalis* or *L. spica*, is pale blue and up to 40 in (1 m) tall; 'Hidcote' is deep purple and 16 in (40 cm) tall; 'Dwarf Blue', dark blue, 16 in (40 cm); 'Munstead', lavender-blue; 'Rosea', pale pink, 16 in (40 cm); 'Nana Alba', white, 12 in (30 cm); *L. × intermedia* 'Grappenhall', medium blue, 32 in (80 cm); 'Hidcote Giant', deep purple, up to 32 in (80 cm) tall; *L. stoechas* (French lavender), deep purple, up to 40 in (1 m); *L. s. pedunculata*, reddish-purple; *L. dentata* (also French lavender), blue-violet.

Lavender flowers are well known for their tremendous fragrance.

Common myrtle
Myrtus communis

The myrtle was common in antiquity. The Greeks dedicated it to the goddess Aphrodite, and also used myrtle branches to adorn their victors in the Olympic Games.

In the Middle East, powdered myrtle leaves are used as baby powder. Because of its antibiotic action, the myrtle is also regarded as a medicinal plant, and drunk as a tea to treat coughs.

The Romans, who paid more attention to worldly enjoyments, regarded myrtle berries as a delicacy. To this day Italian cuisine includes recipes using fresh or dried myrtle berries.

On the continent, the myrtle is still thought of as a symbol of virginity, and a myrtle wreath is regarded as the best wreath for a young bride to wear.

Myrtus communis is a plant of the maquis — the coastal scrub that is so typical of the Mediterranean area, and which only supports plants with very modest requirements. Myrtles flourish on poor, lime-free soils. In the wild they grow into large bushes up to 5 ft (1.5 m) tall. They have small evergreen leaves with an aromatic scent, and delicate white flowers with pronounced yellow stamens, followed by black berries.

Myrtle leaves come in a variety of shapes. The many cultivars include some with nicely variegated leaves. Myrtles are easy to grow, and look most effective if you give them enough space to grow unrestricted.

*The flowers of the common myrtle (*Myrtus communis*)*

Flowering: June–August.

Situation: Sunny to semi-shaded, sheltered.

Growing medium: Humus-rich, free-draining and slightly acid.

Watering/feeding: Water moderately during the growing season (the root ball mustn't dry out); feed moderately but regularly until August.

Routine care: Remove the growing points if you're growing it as a spherical bush.

Overwintering: Cool and light, 41–50°F (5–10°C); water only sparingly.

Pests: Scale insects, aphids.

Special notes: Tolerant of pruning; and can reach a very great age.

Subspecies/cultivars: *M. c. tarentina*, narrow leaves, white fruit; *M. c.* 'Variegata', creamy-edged leaves.

Oleander
Nerium oleander

Oleander has been known for over 2,000 years, and is thought of as one of the classic container plants of Mediterranean origin, first reaching Britain in 1596. By the middle of the last century a large number of cultivars had been developed.

Oleander ranges in the wild from the eastern Mediterranean to the Atlantic coast. It comes in many shapes and forms, but is most commonly seen as a large, bushy shrub that in its natural habitat can easily grow above

An oleander in full flower is invariably a great attraction.

20 ft (6 m). It forms a broad crown with narrow, leathery grey-green leaves. The species has unscented single pink flowers, but some cultivars have flowers that are double or variously scented. The flowers appear in umbels made up of individual flowers, each measuring between 1 in (2 cm) and 3 in (7 cm) in diameter.

About 40 cultivars are available in Britain today, with flowers ranging from single to double, and from white via pale pink to dark red. There are also some salmon-coloured and yellow-flowered forms.

The oleander loves warmth and its flowers enjoy the sun, but its roots like to stand in water. In open countryside you can often find oleanders beside rivers, where their roots burrow their way through the chalky pebbles along the river bed. But take care: as a container plant, oleander can stand waterlogging only during the summer — never in its winter quarters!

Flowering: June–September.

Situation: Full sun; sheltered from rain.

Growing medium: Loamy, humus-rich, chalky.

Watering/feeding: Water copiously during the growing season and feed once a week.

Routine care: Never remove wilted flower-shoots: they form the basis for next year's flowers.

Overwintering: Light, cool, just frost-free; water very sparingly.

Pests/diseases: Aphids, red spider mites, oleander canker.

Special notes: All parts of the plant are extremely poisonous!

Cultivars: Up to 40 different cultivars are commercially available, in many colours and with double and single flowers; there is a dwarf form, which arose as a mutation in Hiroshima.

Pomegranate
Punica granatum

Pomegranates are typical Mediterranean plants, having been cultivated since ancient times. They are mentioned in the Old Testament, and were just as important for the Egyptians as they later became for the Romans and even the early Christians. The Romans brought them north of the Alps, where they were cultivated along with fig trees and Seville oranges.

The pomegranate is not only very powerful as a religious symbol, but the fruits are just as important in the secular world, where they are esteemed both for their culinary value and for the delicious juices that can be obtained from the seeds.

Pomegranates grow into tall shrubs with thorny branches and glossy leaves. The flowers are red in the species, and white, yellow or red in the cultivars. The fruits are spherical in shape with a thick, leathery skin and a distinctively coloured calyx; they contain seeds surrounded by a pulp.

Flowering: Summer.

Situation: Sunny.

Growing medium: Loamy, humus-rich.

Watering/feeding: Water freely until early August; feed until mid-July.

Overwintering: Frost-free, very cool, airy, light or dark.

Pests: Aphids.

Special notes: If you want the plants to fruit, then in the autumn you must remove all the weak shoots from the previous year's growth and shorten the strong shoots. Flowers will then form on the young shoots. It's important for the wood to ripen well, which is why you should stop feeding in mid-July.

Varieties/cultivars: *P. g.* var. *nana* is a dwarf form of the tree, flowering on two-year-old wood. *P. g.* 'Flore Pleno Rubro' has double red flowers, while *P. g.* 'Flore Pleno Luteo' has double yellow flowers; height up to 24 in (60 cm).

*The dwarf pomegranate (*Punica granatum *var.* nana) *goes beautifully in this terracotta pot.*

Rosemary

Rosmarinus officinalis

Rosemary was probably the first Mediterranean plant to penetrate north of the Alps. Nobody knows exactly when rosemary reached northern Europe, but it was listed in Charlemagne's *capitulare de villis.*

Rosemary has always had great symbolic significance as a token of friendship and love. It was originally used for bridal wreaths, and was only later replaced by myrtle. Rosemary was also used in religious

Rosemary is well known as a culinary herb, but here it's being grown as a shrub.

ceremonies in the belief that it could drive away evil spirits.

People were quick to recognise its great medicinal value. Sickrooms and hospitals were at one time 'disinfected' by burning branches of rosemary. It has also been used as a heart stimulant (Greek students wore rosemary wreaths during examinations), as an anti-spasmodic and for the purpose of rejuvenating the skin.

Fresh rosemary flowers were used in the preparation of the famous perfume *aqua reginae hungariae.* Even today rosemary oil, along with other aromatic oils, forms a constituent of many perfumes.

Rosemary today is known primarily as a culinary herb rather than for its medicinal purposes. It is one of the main herbs used in Mediterranean dishes. Although mainly used for seasoning meat and fish dishes, it can also be incorporated in sweet foods.

Rosemary, like the rock rose and myrtle, is an evergreen shrub from the coastal maquis. It has grey-green needle-shaped leaves, and its habit varies from prostrate to bushy and over 6 ft (2 m) tall. Grown in a container, however, it will not grow above 3 ft (1 m).

Flowering: Spring, and often again in the autumn.

Situation: Full sun, hot.

Growing medium: Loamy, rich in humus with extra sand, free-draining.

Rosemary looks really beautiful when in flower, and the leaves give off a delicious aroma.

Watering/feeding: Not much water and very little fertiliser.

Routine care: If necessary, cut back new growth after flowering has finished.

Diseases: Rare.

Special notes: Can't stand waterlogging.

Species/cultivars: *R. officinalis*, pale blue; *R. o.* 'Sissinghurst Blue', dark blue; *R. o.* 'Tuscan Blue', medium blue, broader leaves; *R. o.* 'Severn Sea', strongly scented.

The laurustinus produces lovely fragrant blossoms, but is also greatly valued for its foliage.

Laurustinus
Viburnum tinus

One of the first Mediterranean plants to come into flower is the laurustinus, whose common name reflects its similarity to the bay laurel. Botanically, however, it is a member of the large genus *Viburnum*, which includes a great variety of garden shrubs, many of them native to Britain. The laurustinus was introduced to Britain as early as 1560. It is mainly valued for its fine pink-and-white flowers, which appear in the late winter, and also for its glossy dark-green foliage.

Flowering: Late winter to spring.

Situation: Sun to semi-shade.

Growing medium: Loamy and humus-rich, free-draining.

Watering/feeding: Water only moderately; feed regularly until late July.

Routine care: To keep the plant bushy, pinch out the growing point several times. If a plant grows too big, cut it back hard.

Diseases: Rare.

Overwintering: Very cool, light; can be left outside for a long time; good ventilation essential.

Special notes: Berries are metallic blue; the plant can live to a great age.

Cultivars: *V. t. lucidum* 'Eve Price', buds almost red; *V. t.* 'Gwenllian', dark-pink buds.

Flowering: Spring.

Situation: Sun, though better in semi-shade.

Growing medium: Any normal garden soil.

Watering/feeding: On hot summer days, water the plant and spray the foliage, though not in direct sunlight, to avoid scorching.

Routine care: A regular light trim to keep the plant in good shape.

Overwintering: If temperatures drop below 14°F (−10°C), stand in a frost-free position and water only sparingly, but don't let the plant dry out.

Pests: Scale insects, box tree gall midges.

A box trained into a spherical bush is a beautiful sight.

Species/cultivars: *B. sempervirens* 'Suffruticosa', a very slow-growing dwarf form; *B. s.* 'Latifolia Maculata', a golden-leaved cultivar with bronze autumn tints; *B. s.* 'Aurea Marginata', with narrow yellow-edged leaves; *B. s.* 'Handsworthiensis', upright habit, ideal for tall shapes; *B. microphylla* 'Faulkner', a small, very hardy shrub with fresh-green foliage.

Green-leaved evergreens

There are two further elements that should be included in a Mediterranean-style patio display. These are firstly plants with attractively shaped leaves, and secondly evergreen plants with thick foliage that is tolerant of pruning.

Apart from a few very notable exceptions, the flowers on such plants tend to be small and inconspicuous, playing rather a subordinate role compared with the leaves.

Box
Buxus
Box is one of the most important of the evergreen plants, and makes an excellent backdrop for a summer flower display. Its great popularity owes much to the fact that it can be clipped into every conceivable shape. Box is a slow-growing, fairly undemanding plant and that can be very long-lived. Its small, glossy dark-green leaves give off a characteristic aroma.

Bay laurel, sweet bay
Laurus nobilis
There must be few plants that are so wreathed in legend as the bay laurel — a classic plant of the Mediterranean area. Its original home is Italy, but its history is closely linked with Ancient Greece. The Greeks

dedicated it to Apollo, and decorated their temples with sprigs of laurel. The Romans crowned their victors with it. Centuries later, in the Renaissance, poets were again honoured with laurel wreaths. In all Western cultures, being crowned with laurel was a very special honour.

North of the Alps, the laurel became known early in the Middle Ages, and was valued mainly for its medicinal powers. Only later did it come to be grown for decorative purposes.

Laurel grows quickly in favourable situations, and in its natural habitat it can grow as tall as 33 ft (10 m). The leaves are dark green and pointed at the tips. The little yellow flowers appear in umbels and are followed by black berries.

Flowering: Spring.

Situation: Sunny.

Growing medium: Loamy and humus-rich with some added sand, free-draining.

Watering/feeding: Don't let the root ball dry out; feed once a week until August.

Overwintering: Cool, light, airy; doesn't like frost.

Pests: Scale insects.

Special notes: When pruning, take care to cut *between* the leaves, as the leaves don't look very attractive when cut.

It takes years of patience to train a bay laurel like this.

Mahonia
Mahonia

Mahonias make impressive container plants, some of them growing very vigorously. The compound leaves are extremely attractive, being long, lustrous and very prickly. But even these pale by comparison with those gorgeous clusters of yellow flowers. These appear at various times during the winter, depending on the cultivar, and generally have a strong scent. The blue-black fruits provide an additional attraction.

Mahonias come from eastern Asia, but adapt well to the British climate provided you give them a spot in the shade or semi-shade.

The blue fruits of the mahonia

The mahonia provides a magnificent display of yellow flowers.

Flowering: November–May, depending on species and cultivar.

Situation: Semi-shade to shade.

Growing medium: Rich in humus, free-draining.

Feeding/watering: Water and feed in moderation.

Routine care: Undemanding.

Overwintering: Hardy down to 5°F (-15°C) if protected, but better in a frost-free location.

Diseases: Rare.

Special notes: Prickly leaves, blue berries.

Species/cultivars: *M. lomariifolia*, golden-yellow flowers in large, upright racemes; *M. × media* 'Winter Sun', strongly scented; *M. × m.* 'Buckland', primrose-yellow; *M. × m.* 'Charity', bright yellow.

Grey-leaved evergreens

Plants with grey foliage give a patio a very distinctive Mediterranean character. Grey comes in many shades in the natural world (think of all the nuances of stone colours), all of which make a very welcome addition to a garden or patio display. Plants with grey foliage provide a pleasantly exotic yet neutral background to a planting scheme of brightly coloured plants from countries with a warmer climate than ours.

Rue has attractively divided grey-green leaves.

Cotton lavender has lovely yellow flowers.

Common rue
Ruta graveolens
Rue, a native of the Mediterranean area, is a medicinal plant. Its leaves are unusually deeply divided, giving it great decorative value.

Flowering: Summer.

Situation: Sunny.

Growing medium: Humus-rich; very free-draining.

Watering/feeding: Water and feed in moderation.

Routine care: Cut back after flowering.

Overwintering: Cool, light, frost-free.

Diseases: Rare.

Special notes: Contact with the sap can cause skin rashes and burns, so be careful when handling common rue.

Cultivars: *R. g.* 'Jackman's Blue' 16–32 in (40–80 cm); *R. g.* 'Variegata' 16–32 in (40–80 cm).

Cotton lavender
Santolina
In its natural habitat this plant grows to form wide bushes. The delicately structured, silvery foliage makes it the ideal background for a collection of Mediterranean container plants. The leaves have a pungent scent that was once used as a moth or insect repellent.

Flowering: July–August.

Situation: Sunny.

Growing medium: Free-draining, lean, chalky.

Watering/feeding: Water in moderation, and feed only very little.

Routine care: Cut back after flowering.

Overwintering: Cool, just frost-free, dry and not dark.

Diseases: Rare.

Special notes: The plant quickly becomes woody.

Species/Cultivars: *S. chamaecyparissus* var. *nana*, low-growing bushes with grey-green foliage; *S. pinnata neapolitana* 'Edward Bowles', delicately structured silvery foliage and golden-yellow flowers; *S. serratifolia*, grey foliage and lemon-yellow flowers.

From the tropics and subtropics

Plants from the tropical and subtropical regions of the earth have totally different requirements from the Mediterranean-type plants that have been described so far.

These plants can be divided into two main categories. Firstly there are plants from tropical

mountain ranges, where precipitation is high, while temperatures are very warm in the daytime but very cool at night. Then there are those plants that flourish in damp but more equable regions, either near major expanses of water or on the windward side of mountain ranges. The plants in both these groups like high humidity levels and predominantly acid soil.

This patio is full of gorgeous tropical plants in full bloom.

Abutilons are noted for their remarkable and unusual flowers.

Abutilon
Abutilon
Abutilons are small evergreen or semi-evergreen shrubs that originate in tropical mountain ranges. They are highly valued for their unusually shaped flowers, and some species will stay in flower all year round.

There are a number of species that make interesting container plants. They are relatively easy to look after, and are particularly suitable for growing as standards.

Flowering: All year round.

Situation: Sun to semi-shade; plenty of light but avoid direct midday sun.

Growing medium: Rich in humus and nutrients, but low in lime.

Watering/feeding: Always keep moist; feed once a week.

Routine care: Deadhead regularly; cut back in the autumn or late winter.

Overwintering: Well lit; frost-free but not too warm at around 50°F (10°C). Water sparingly.

Pests/diseases: Aphids, red spider mites, grey mould (*Botrytis*); flowers drop if temperatures fluctuate.

Special notes: Demands plenty of light and doesn't like rain very much.

Species/cultivars: *A. megapotamicum,* pendent habit, thin shoots, narrow maple-like leaves, yellow flowers with red sepals and violet stamens; *A. m.* 'Variegatum', like the species but with yellow-variegated foliage; *A. × milleri*, light-yellow flowers with orange calyxes; *A.* 'Boule de Neige', white flowers; *A.* 'Fireball', red flowers; *A. vitifolium*, lavender-blue flowers; *A. v. album*, white flowers.

Lemon verbena
Aloysia triphylla
This plant is a real must for all fragrance fetishists. At the very slightest touch, its fresh-green leaves give off streams of intense lemon fragrance.

Lemon verbena isn't grown very much today, but in the 19th century it was very commonly grown in cottage gardens. It is nowadays grown commercially in France, where an essential oil from the leaves is used as a raw ingredient in cosmetics. The fragrant foliage can be dried to make a delicious and refreshing tea.

Flowering: Summer.

Situation: Sunny.

Growing medium: Rich in humus and nutrients, loamy.

Watering/feeding: Water freely when in full growth, but only feed if you're using the plant for ornamental purposes.

Routine care: Can be trimmed in the autumn.

Overwintering: Frost-free, very cool, also dark.

Diseases: Rare.

Lemon verbena has small flowers but is noted for its fragrance.

Cassia
Cassia and *Senna*

Some 600 different species of cassia are to be found in the tropics and subtropics, including some of the most beautiful yellow-flowered shrubs. They also make extremely attractive container plants, with their compound pinnate leaves and spikes of yellow flowers.

Cassias can appear in many different forms, ranging from trees to bushes with hanging branches and pendent flower clusters. Their requirements are correspondingly varied.

The tropical cassia is one of the classic container plants.

Most of the cassias available in Britain have been reassigned to the botanical genus *Senna*. An exception is the tree-like *Cassia javanica*, with its pink flowers.

Flowering: Summer to late autumn (all year round in a conservatory).

Situation: Sunny.

Growing medium: Rich in humus and nutrients; nicely moist but not waterlogged.

Watering/feeding: Water freely when in full growth; feed once a week until August.

Routine care: Cut back before bringing indoors for the winter.

Overwintering: Species vary in requirements, but most need to be kept frost-free, and in no case should the root ball be allowed to dry out. *Senna marilandica* is the most robust and can stand a few degrees of frost; overwinter dark but not too damp. *S. corymbosa* also tolerates slight frost; overwinter dark. *S. didymobotrya* (golden wonder) is the most delicate: overwinter in light and never below 50°F (10°C).

Pests/diseases: Aphids, grey mould (*Botrytis*).

Species/cultivars: *S. artemisi-oides* (silver cassia, wormwood cassia) is good for poor soils and a dry climate; it forms bushes, which become covered in yellow flowers. *S. corymbosa* bears large, intensely yellow flowers on every branch, and flowers as early as June. *S. didy-mobotrya* is strongly aromatic, bearing large flower spikes and leaves with many leaflets.

Cestrum
Cestrum

This semi-evergreen plant from tropical South America is yet another must for a tropical-style patio. But if you want it to flower in summer (it flowers in winter in its native habitat), you have to interfere with its natural cycle. Bring the plant indoors before the first frosts and immediately remove the inflorescences that have already formed. It forms new flower shoots, but only after it has overwintered. After this treatment, flowering

28

A red-flowered cestrum in full bloom makes a glorious display.

The leaves and flowers of the Mexican orange blossom give off a beautiful scent.

should last right through the summer until autumn. Cestrums have hanging branches covered with long-lasting umbels of flowers, and can reach heights of 5–10 ft (1.5–3 m).

Flowering: Summer to autumn.

Situation: Sunny.

Growing medium: Rich in humus and nutrients.

Watering/feeding: Water and feed freely and regularly.

Routine care: Support standard forms well, and protect them from wind.

Overwintering: Frost-free, cool; either light, airy and nearly dry, or dark (but then cut them back almost to the ground). Should be kept warmer in a conservatory in order to stimulate flowering.

Pests/diseases: Aphids, grey mould (*Botrytis*); non-woody stems and leaves can rot during rainy periods in the summer.

Special notes: All cestrums are poisonous!

Species/cultivars: *C. aurantiacum*, yellow flowers, later orange, on bare wood in winter; *C. elegans*, very varied, growing up to 10 ft (3 m), evergreen, very large purplish-red flowers and dark-red fleshy berries; *C.* 'Newellii', overhanging branches and light-red flowers; *C. nocturnum*, night-scented species with pale-yellow flowers; *C. parqui*, the hardiest, will overwinter outside in mild areas, and bears pale-yellow flowers.

Mexican orange blossom
Choisya ternata

Mexican orange blossom is so named because it is related to the citrus plants and has orange-scented flowers. It is probably one of the least demanding of all the tropical plants. Even in a container it will grow into a dense and attractive bush with decoratively fan-shaped dark-green leaves.

Flowering: Spring to early summer.

Situation: Sun to semi-shade.

Growing medium: Rich in humus and nutrients — free-draining but not too dry.

Watering/feeding: Water and feed freely.

Overwintering: Very cool and light; tolerates slight frost.

Pests: Red spider mites.

Special notes: Tolerates some pruning; can also be trained into a spherical bush, but then it won't flower.

A fine specimen of angel's trumpet

Growing medium: Very rich in nutrients, loamy, water-retentive without becoming waterlogged.

Watering/feeding: Water freely every day; feed twice a week.

Routine care: Provide support if necessary.

Overwintering: Frost-free, cool, 40–50°F (4–10°C); light (or dark and almost dry if you cut them hard back); the cooler, the drier.

Pests: Aphids, leaf bugs, red spider mites.

Special notes: You can plant angel's trumpet out in the garden for the summer. All parts of the plant are poisonous.

Angel's trumpet
Brugmansia

These plants are so well known that there is virtually no need to introduce them. Next to olean-der, they are possibly the most popular container plant.

Until recently, the angel's trumpet belonged to the botani-cal genus *Datura* — a name derived from an Indian word meaning 'thorn-apple' (which nicely describes the fruits). However, the majority of angel's trumpet species have now been reassigned to the new genus *Brugmansia*.

The most helpful way of dividing the species is by their habit. The weaker-growing *B. sanguinea* is often named *B. rosei*; this species flowers from September until April, so is only suitable for a warm greenhouse. *B. suaveolens*, the best-known species, is one of the moderate-ly vigorous group; *B. × candida* is similar. *B. aurea* is a vigorous species with enormous leaves, so needs lots of space.

Flowering: Summer, in batches.

Situation: Sunny, sheltered from wind.

Species/cultivars: *B. sangui-nea*, red flowers with yellow centres, 8 in (20 cm) long, unscented; *B. suaveolens*, white flowers angled downwards, 12 in (30 cm) long, strongly scented; *B. × candida* 'Knightii', white hanging flowers; *B. aurea*, white to apricot in colour.

Scented-leaved pelargoniums
Pelargonium

These aren't the most colourful of container plants, but they are still very popular on account of their attractive foliage and especially their fragrance. They originated in South Africa, and are very closely related to the pelargoniums that are grown for their flowers.

Only a few of the most interesting scented-leaved pelargoniums are given here, as there are so many species and varieties, each with its own distinctive leaf shape and scent. The most notable of them is the rose pelargonium (*P.* 'Graveolens'), which is so named because its leaves provide an essential oil that is used in the perfume industry as a substitute for the genuine (but very expensive) rose oil.

Flowering: Spring to late summer.

Situation: Sun to semi-shade, depending on the cultivar.

Growing medium: Humus-rich, light, free-draining.

Watering/feeding: During the growth period, give a weak feed once a fortnight and water only moderately; avoid waterlogging.

Routine care: Never prune in spring or they won't flower.

Overwintering: Frost-free, cool and light (never dark); water very sparingly; overwinter young plants at around 54°F (12°C).

Pests: Occasionally aphids.

Special notes: Some species develop branching shoots that you can shorten after flowering.

Species/cultivars: *P.* 'Graveolens' (rose pelargonium), up to 3 ft (1 m), very large, deeply lobed, hairy grey-green leaves, delicate-pink flowers; *P. tomentosum* (peppermint geranium), widely spreading, large emerald-green leaves, tiny white flowers; *P.* 'Fragrans', pine-scented, satiny grey-green leaves, small white flowers; *P. crispum* 'Variegatum', lemon-scented, two-coloured leaves with crinkled edges, pink flowers; *P.* 'Mabel Grey', strongly lemon-scented, light-green divided leaves, mauve flowers with red stripes; *P.* 'Prince of Orange', smelling of oranges, deeply divided leaves, large pink flowers, suitable for growing as a standard.

An assortment of scented-leaved pelargoniums

The cockspur coral tree produces some of the most magnificent flowers of any plant.

40–46°F; 5–8°C); always keep it absolutely dry.

Pests: Red spider mites.

Special notes: Don't prune when in full growth as the new shoots are needed for flowering.

Species/cultivars: *E. c.* 'Compacta' flowers even as a young plant. The species won't flower until quite large, and requires a large container.

Cockspur coral tree
Erythrina crista-galli
The cockspur coral tree is one of the most beautiful flowering shrubs of the tropics and sub-tropics. It comes originally from subtropical South America.

This plant has thick, woody, often thorny shoots, and bears clusters of magnificent scarlet flowers — a single flower can measure as much as 2 in (5 cm) in length.

Flowering: Early summer to late autumn, in batches.

Situation: Sunny.

Growing medium: Rich in humus and nutrients, free-draining.

Watering/feeding: Water freely when in full growth, and feed once a week.

Overwintering: Keep plant dark and frost-free (at around

Japanese aralia
Fatsia japonica
This aralia is familiar to many as a houseplant. With its large, fan-shaped leaves, *Fatsia japonica* makes a very striking container plant. It develops outstandingly well, particularly in shaded situations, and makes an ideal plant for a town garden.

The Japanese aralia comes from the Far East, where it grows chiefly in the coastal

The Japanese aralia is a plant that likes the shade

woodlands of Japan and Korea. It has long been cultivated in Japanese gardens, where a number of cultivars are grown that have not so far been introduced into Britain.

Fatsia japonica is a large-leaved plant. Its glossy deep-green leaves are deeply lobed, leathery and borne on long stalks; they can grow as large as 10×16 in (25×40 cm). The highly decorative foliage forms an exotic-looking background to the dense clusters of cream-coloured flowers, which appear in the autumn. The little black berries provide further adornment in November.

Flowering: Late summer to autumn.

Situation: Shade (also semi-shade if there's enough water).

Growing medium: Rich in humus and nutrients.

Watering/feeding: Water freely during the summer; feed only sparingly; avoid waterlogging.

Overwintering: Hardy down to 14°F (−10°C).

Diseases: Stem and root rot.

Cultivars: *F.j.* 'Variegata', creamy-variegated foliage.

Hebe
Hebe
As well as making excellent garden plants, the many species and cultivars of *Hebe* are also extremely good as container plants. Most hebes have narrow green or grey-green foliage,

Hebe *flowers appear in late summer and remain attractive for a long time.*

accompanied by attractive clusters of white, blue-violet, pink or crimson flowers. These plants vary greatly in size, ranging from a few inches to several feet tall.

Flowering: Summer to autumn.

Situation: Sunny.

Growing medium: Rich in humus and nutrients, free-draining.

Watering/feeding: Keep nicely moist when in full growth, but avoid waterlogging; feed once a fortnight.

Overwintering: Cool and light (ideal for a cool greenhouse); water only sparingly. Some hebes are hardy enough to overwinter outside.

Diseases: Extremely prone to fungal attack if kept in a damp situation.

Species/cultivars: *H.* 'La Séduisante', a spherical bush bearing clusters of brilliant-crimson flowers in late summer; *H.* 'Alicia Amherst' has a spreading habit and bears blue-violet flowers in summer; *H.* 'Great Orme', bearing fragrant browny-pink flowers from spring to autumn; *H.* 'Midsummer Beauty', fragrant light-blue flowers in summer.

33

Hibiscus rosa-sinensis

Rose of China
Hibiscus rosa-sinensis
This plant probably originated in China, but it has since spread throughout the world. There are innumerable varieties, especially on Sri Lanka and the Pacific islands. Its blooms are the very embodiment of the 'tropical flower', and Hawaii's national flower, the Hawaiian hibiscus, is a variety of *H. rosa-sinensis*.

In order to flower, this plant needs a moist tropical climate with temperatures of 62–83°F (17–28°C). In Britain you'll have a lot of trouble persuading it to flower. It needs warm, very humid conditions out of the direct sun — a very difficult combination to achieve. But the wonderfully exotic blooms will make it well worth the attempt.

Flowering: Summer.

Situation: Sunny, humid.

Growing medium: Humus-rich, with loam and silicate.

Watering/feeding: Water and feed freely; don't let the root ball dry out, but avoid waterlogging.

Routine care: Cut back every other year to keep it bushy.

Overwintering: Frost-free, not below 54°F (12°C); light and airy; water only in moderation.

Pests/diseases: Aphids, woolly aphids, red spider mites, fungal attack.

Special notes: Needs plenty of light.

Species/cultivars: Many cultivars in all colours. The closely related *H. syriacus* requires less demanding conditions.

The flowers of the crape myrtle

Crape myrtle
Lagerstroemia indica
If you visit southern Europe in August, you'll often see these small trees in parks or along the roadside. The tips of their upright branches have thick tufts of flowers up to 8 in (20 cm) long. The crape myrtle is relatively hardy, and is therefore one of the most popular of all flowering trees and shrubs.

Flowering: August to October.

Position: Sunny and hot (or it flowers too late); sheltered.

Growing medium: Rich in humus and nutrients, rather sandy, very free-draining.

Watering/feeding: Never allow the root ball to dry out or the flowers will drop; water freely when in full growth but avoid waterlogging; feed once a week until September.

Routine care: If you want to train it as a tree, prune it like a standard before bringing it in for the winter. For a bush, train just a few strong shoots.

Overwintering: In mild, sheltered areas, it's frost-hardy down to 5°F (-15°C). In cold or exposed areas, overwinter very cool, dark and almost dry.

Pests/diseases: Aphids, mildew.

Special notes: Crape myrtles sprout very late, but don't let this bother you. You must cut them back, as they flower only at the tips of the young shoots. They are also liable to break.

Cultivars: Various cultivars with white, pink, violet or red flowers. The red cultivars are the least free-flowering. There is a dwarf form, which grows only 32 in (80 cm) tall.

Lantana
Lantana
These evergreen plants hardly need any introduction. They come originally from tropical America and Africa, where they are often regarded as weeds.

In this country they are grown either as bedding or as container plants. They bear hosts of little flowers that combine to form small hemispherical heads — and they have sturdy deep-green foliage that gives off a pungent aroma.

Flowering: Summer through to autumn.

Situation: Sunny.

Growing medium: Rich in humus and nutrients, loamy.

Watering/feeding: Water and feed in moderation; avoid waterlogging.

Routine care: Shorten the shoots to about half their length every spring.

Overwintering: Frost-free, cool and light, almost dry.

Pests: Red spider mites.

Special notes: Flowers change colour; berries are metallic blue and poisonous.

Species/cultivars: Only very few of the 150 different species are commonly grown as container plants: *L. montevidensis*, low-growing and bushy, with rose-lilac flowers and crimson autumn colouring; *L. camara* hybrids, with flowers in lots of different colours.

Lantanas make particularly fine standards.

Osmanthus

This genus of evergreen plants is native to southeast Asia. The most typical species have small, leathery dark-green leaves and white tufts of flowers borne on overhanging branches. The strongly scented flowers appear some time between March and mid-May, depending on the situation, and on the species or cultivar. *Osmanthus* species are highly adaptable plants, flourishing in both sunny and semi-shaded sites.

Flowering: Spring, summer or autumn, depending on the species or cultivar.

Situation: Sun to semi-shade.

Osmanthus *blooms fill the whole garden with their scent.*

Growing medium: Rich in humus and nutrients, free-draining.

Watering/feeding: Water and feed in moderation; keep the root ball moist but avoid any waterlogging.

Overwintering: Most are hardy down to 5°F (-15°C) and can be overwintered outside.

Pests: Aphids, scale insects.

Special notes: Strongly scented; foliage and speed of growth differ greatly between species.

Species/cultivars: *O. delavayi*, small leaves, white flowers similar to jasmine; *O. × burkwoodii*, somewhat more robust than *O. delavayi*; *O. fragrans* (fragrant olive), bears white flowers in autumn; *O. heterophyllus*, dark-green holly-like foliage, flowers in late autumn (there are several variegated cultivars); *O. decorus*, glossy foliage, white flowers in late spring.

Pittosporum
Pittosporum

The genus *Pittosporum* contains about 150 species, which vary greatly in appearance. These beautiful evergreen trees and shrubs come from the tropics and subtropics, and are very fragrant in the summer. They are undemanding plants, grown for their attractive glossy green foliage and their fragrant white flowers. Some species have sticky seeds.

Flowering: Spring to early summer.

Situation: Sunny.

Growing medium: Rich in nutrients and humus.

Overwintering: Moderately hardy, but better kept frost-free, light and airy; can also be overwintered dark, but must then be kept very cool or the leaves will drop.

Pests: Aphids, scale insects.

Special notes: Tolerant of pruning, fragrant.

Species/cultivars: The main differences between the various species and cultivars are in the foliage. *P. tobira* (Japanese pittosporum), glossy dark-green foliage, vigorous habit, white flowers; *P. tobira* 'Nanum', low-growing, white flowers;

Pittosporum *flowers are also wonderfully scented.*

P. tenuifolium, the most popular species, wavy-edged leaves, dark-red flowers; *P. tenuifolium* 'Silver Queen', white-variegated foliage; *P. undulatum* (Victorian box), wavy-edged leaves, white flowers; *P. crassifolium* (karo), red flowers.

Glory bush

Tibouchina urvilleana
Tibouchina is a genus of over 200 species, all of them native to tropical America. But only *T. urvilleana* is of interest as a container plant. In the wild, the glory bush grows into a 20-ft (6-m) tree. In a container it can also reach a considerable size under favourable conditions, provided you don't prune it.
The glory bush is cultivated mainly for its magnificent blue-purple flowers, which last from the end of September well into the autumn. The soft, velvety leaves are a particularly decorative feature, and take on a reddish colour as the temperatures fall in late autumn.

Flowering: Late summer to autumn.

Situation: Sunny.

Growing medium: Rich in humus and nutrients, free-draining.

Watering/feeding: Water and feed regularly when in full growth.

Routine care: You can keep the plant bushy by pruning, but you should only prune while it's in full growth, and only cut into wood up to one year old.

The glory bush is a magnificent sight with its gorgeous flowers and velvety foliage.

Pruning can also be a useful way of regulating the flowering season: if left unpruned, the plant starts flowering in high summer.

Overwintering: Frost-free, not below 41°F (5°C); light; water sparingly.

Diseases: Rare; virus infection of the roots if waterlogged.

Special notes: Very easily becomes squarrose.

Species/cultivars: The species bears large blue-purple flowers in late summer; the dwarf form flowers in a rather darker blue, but because it does so as late as December, it's only suitable for conservatories.

Climbers

Climbers can perform a very useful role in a garden, either dividing a space up or helping to give a sense of space. And on a balcony or patio they perform the equally important task of providing a screen.

However, climbers shouldn't just be thought of as useful plants. They have great decorative value too, and in a small space they make the ideal alternative to shrubs and trees. Climbers invariably create a pleasantly intimate atmosphere — and even the most desolate inner-city balcony can be turned into a cosy bower by the judicious addition of a few exotic climbing plants.

Of course, climbers in containers are bound not to reach the full size of those grown in open ground. But that's only natural, and it's certainly no reason for rejecting climbers out of hand.

To save yourself trouble and annoyance, there are a few important things to note before you start choosing any climbers. The most important question to consider is the situation and aspect of your patio or balcony. How much sun does it get each day? Is it exposed to cold northerly or easterly winds?

You also need to think about which side of the plant is going to be exposed to the weather, particularly in areas subject to heavy summer thunderstorms. 'Ordinary' container plants can

be pushed around a little from place to place (although they don't really it like it much). But once your climbers are in place, they have to stay put.

The next consideration is no less important, and that is the supporting framework. The majority of climbers need one right from the very beginning. Depending on what plant you choose, the support must be sufficiently strong and stable to hold the plant as it grows bigger. You don't want it to collapse a year later under the weight of new branches. Any later alteration to the support is usually difficult to achieve, and is always at the plant's expense.

The same applies to the pot. You not only need to choose the right container, but you need to be able to predict the correct size for the plant when it's fully grown. Once a climber has grown into the pot, you can't usually repot it without damaging it.

Overwintering climbers isn't always a simple procedure either. Once the plant has twined itself round the support, you can only transfer it to its winter quarters together with its support. But there is one crumb of comfort: many of the more exotic specimens usually have to be cut back before being brought indoors, which means they can be moved to another site without any problem.

Bougainvillea
Bougainvillea

The genus *Bougainvillea* has without doubt provided us with some of the most striking and attractive of all container plants. These plants come originally from the tropical regions of Asia and the Pacific.

Botanically speaking, the 'flowers' are bracts, or modified leaves surrounding the tiny flowers proper. They come in lots of different colours, and if you choose the right species or cultivars, you can have colour all through the summer.

B. glabra, with its reddish-violet bracts, is the most robust of all the bougainvilleas, and is therefore the most suitable for growing in containers.

Flowering: Summer.

Left *Bougainvilleas are among the most luxuriant of plants, and this one is a particularly fine specimen.*

Situation: Sunny, sheltered from wind.

Growing medium: Rich in nutrients and humus; moist but not waterlogged.

Watering/feeding: Water freely when in full growth and feed once a week.

Routine care: Shorten the long shoots as they form.

Overwintering: Frost-free, cool and somewhat dry. Don't let the root ball get cold and wet at the same time — if you accidentally overwater a plant, move it quickly into a warm room.

Pests/diseases: Aphids, caterpillars, mildew.

Cultivars: Many different cultivars of *B. glabra* are readily available.

They look less impressive in a pot, but the flowers are still amazing.

The large flowers of the trumpet creeper

Trumpet creeper or trumpet vine
Campsis

The trumpet creeper is a fast-growing creeper that grows to 16 ft (5 m) in favourable situations. The large panicles of trumpet-shaped flowers appear in a tremendous variety of colours, ranging from light yellow to scarlet. The shoots are strong and branching — the leaves light green and pinnate.

Flowering: July–September.

Situation: Sunny.

Growing medium: Rich in humus and nutrients, free-draining.

Watering/feeding: Water freely and feed regularly when in full growth.

Routine care: Cut back flower shoots in late autumn or spring.

Overwintering: Hardy down to –4°F (–20°C).

Pests: Aphids, red spider mites.

Special notes: Flowers appear at the tips of young shoots; needs a warm wall in order to flower well.

Species/cultivars: *C. radicans flava*, yellow; *C. × tagliabuana* 'Mme Galen', coral-red, free-flowering.

Jasmine
Jasminum

Among the most sought-after climbers are the jasmines, whose tropical and subtropical species are valued chiefly for the wonderful fragrance of their flowers. However, their superb, mainly evergreen foliage also makes them extremely attractive as container plants.

All jasmine species need some kind of support, but can be cut back without hesitation. There are lots of different species, and

The flowers and branches of the primrose jasmine

their requirements often vary considerably. But with the exception of *J. nudiflorum* (winter jasmine) and *J. officinale* (common jasmine) they all need frost-free winter quarters.

Flowering: Varies according to species.

Situation: Sun to semi-shade.

Growing medium: Rich in humus and nutrients, free-draining.

Routine care: Cut back if the plant is growing too vigorously.

Watering/feeding: Keep moderately moist and feed regularly.

Overwintering: Varies according to species — some won't tolerate any frost and must overwinter very cool and light.

Diseases: Rare.

Species:

Primrose jasmine (*J. mesnyi*) is one of the winter-flowering species. In a frost-free conservatory its yellow flowers appear in late winter, and with its cascade of overhanging branches it makes a magnificent sight. *J. mesnyi* is only semi-evergreen, and can lose part of its foliage.

If you anticipate temperatures below 14°F (-10°C), you must overwinter the container plant somewhere cool and possibly dark. Prune it immediately after flowering, otherwise there will be no flowers the following year. *J. mesnyi* prefers fresh soil with plenty of humus and nutrients, and an ample supply of water in the spring.

Common jasmine or jessamine (*J. officinale*) is the best-known species. Its native range extends from the Caucasus through to China. It has been used in the perfume industry for centuries, and is grown on a large scale in southern France for this purpose.

J. officinale grows best with plenty of sun, and flourishes in lean soils. In high summer the white flower clusters give off an enchanting evening perfume, more pleasant than that of *J. polyanthum*. *J. officinale* grows vigorously, often to over 30 ft (10 m) in favourable situations. It can also be pruned in the autumn. It is robust, and will tolerate temperatures of 5°F (-15°C) or even lower.

J. polyanthum is native to China. It has intensely green,

attractively pinnate leaves. The white flowers appear in great abundance in the early summer, and start off flushed pink on the outside. Their heady fragrance can be detected a long way off.

J. polyanthum is a strong-growing climber that can easily grow to 16 ft (5 m), but it is sensitive to cold winds (the leaves react by shrivelling). It tolerates some frost, but prefers to overwinter frost-free and light, and is an ideal plant for a conservatory. If it grows too big, you can prune it in the autumn before bringing it indoors. This plant also needs plenty of water and nutrients.

Arabian jasmine (*J. sambac*) from India and Sri Lanka looks very different from any of the species described so far. Its leathery leaves are oval to roundish and arranged in threes.

The white flowers appear in clusters of up to twelve, and are beautifully fragrant. They are used in perfume manufacture and in jasmine-scented teas.

J. sambac grows less vigorously than other jasmines, reaching only 10 ft (3 m), but you can prune it whenever you like. It must be overwintered somewhere cool but frost-free.

Winter jasmine (*J. nudiflorum*) should not be confused with primrose jasmine, which also has yellow flowers. *J. nudiflorum* produces flowers in the late winter on overhanging branches that are still bare of foliage. It is very hardy and undemanding, and can be overwintered in the open.

Common jasmine in full flower

The flowers of the wax mallow are reminiscent of some abutilons.

sunny patio or a warm wall. They can easily be raised from seed, and eventually reach a height of some 25 ft (8 m).

Flowering: June–September.

Situation: Sunny, airy.

Growing medium: Humus-rich, nutrient-rich, free-draining.

Watering/feeding: Water well but avoid waterlogging. Once the plant starts into growth, feed weekly until August.

Routine care: After the leaves drop, cut back to the ground.

Overwintering: Bring the plant indoors with the root ball dry, and overwinter very cool and dark, watering only very sparingly. In March, move your plant to somewhere that is warmer and better lit, and it will send up fresh shoots from the roots again.

Pests/diseases: Aphids and red spider mites; root rot if the root ball remains wet.

Special notes: Poisonous.

Species/cultivars: *M. laxa* (Chilean jasmine), white flowers; *M × amoena* 'Alice du Pont', evergreen, pink flowers, tender.

Mandevilla
Mandevilla

These natives of South America have a bewitching fragrance that is a little reminiscent of jasmine. The species *M. laxa* has the common name Chilean jasmine.

Mandevillas are fast-growing twining climbers with thin stems that contain a milky sap and bear large, fresh-green heart-shaped leaves. The white or pink flowers are borne in clusters and followed by long, bean-like fruits. Mandevillas are easy to grow, and make outstandingly good container plants for a

This bower vine has delicate-pink flowers with darker centres.

Wax mallow
Malvaviscus arboreus

The genus *Malvaviscus* contains some magnificent container plants, whose flowers are a little reminiscent of *Abutilon*. They come originally from Central and South America.

The wax mallow grows fast but won't tolerate any frost. The downy leaves are large and deep green. The red flowers are over 1 in (3 cm) long with protruding stamens, and hang on long stalks.

Flowering: All year round in warm situations.

Situation: Warm, sunny to semi-shaded.

Growing medium: Rich in humus and nutrients.

Watering/feeding: Keep the root ball moist and feed once a week.

Overwintering: Light and completely frost-free (around 50°F; 10°C); water sparingly.

Pests: Aphids, whitefly.

Special notes: Demands lots of light; hardly branches at all, but can be cut back; very suitable for growing as a standard.

Subspecies: *M. a. mexicanus* is the most commonly seen form; it has unlobed leaves.

Mandevilla — a climber with a delicious scent

Bower vine
Pandorea jasminoides

Like the well-known trumpet creeper, the bower vine belongs to the plant family Bignoni-aceae. It is very attractive with its pinnate evergreen leaves and white or pink flowers.

Flowering: June–August.

Situation: Sunny, light.

Growing medium: Rich in humus and nutrients; moist but not waterlogged.

Watering/feeding: When in full growth, keep moist and feed regularly.

Overwintering: Won't tolerate any frost. A light, moderately warm conservatory is ideal, enabling it to start flowering as early as March. If light levels remain too low, the flowers will drop off.

Pests: Aphids.

Cultivars: *P. j.* 'Alba' white; *P. j.* 'Rosea Superba' pink.

The beautiful passion flower

giant granadilla) must be over-wintered somewhere frost-free. The plants' other requirements are similarly varied.

Flowering: Spring to early autumn, depending on species.

Situation: Sunny, very humid.

Growing medium: Rich in nutrients and humus, very free-draining.

Watering/feeding: Water generously, spray occasionally and feed once a week.

Overwintering: In light; norm-ally frost-free, but temperature varies from species to species.

Pests: Aphids, scale insects, woolly aphids, red spider mites.

Special notes: Needs cutting back when brought indoors; support needed.

Passion flower
Passiflora

Of all container plants, *Passi-flora* is probably the one with the most exotic blooms. The passion flower is native to tropi-cal and subtropical America, from where Jesuit missionaries brought it to Europe in the 17th century. According to legend, the features of the flower sym-bolise Christ's crucifixion, which is no doubt how the plant came to be called the passion flower.

The passion flower is also a plant of great medicinal value, based on various active agents that are contained within above-ground parts of the plant and are strongest during the flower-ing period. These substances are very effective in treating stress, insomnia and various nervous complaints. The Native Ameri-cans used to prepare a soporific from *Passiflora* long before the European colonists arrived.

The genus *Passiflora* contains around 500 species of different climbing plants; even experts find them difficult to identify. They're very easy to cross-breed, so there are numerous hybrids that are commercially available. The different species vary considerably in their requirements. Some, like *P. caerulea* (the common passion flower), are very robust, and in mild situations can remain out of doors all year round. Others such as *P. quadrangularis* (the

Species/cultivars: *P. caerulea* (common passion flower), blue/ white/pale-pink flowers, very robust; *P.* 'Constance Elliott', ivory-white flowers; *P.* × *belotti*, lilac-white flowers; *P. violacea*, large, pendent violet-coloured flowers, fast-growing; *P. incar-nata*, white/lavender-coloured flowers followed by edible fruits, late-sprouting, very robust; *P. edulis* (passion fruit), large crimson flowers followed by edible fruits, for warm con-servatories only; *P. racemosa* (red passion flower), scarlet flowers in very large clusters of 8–13 individual flowers (one of the most beautiful species).

Leadwort
Plumbago
This upright or climbing semi-evergreen shrub is an excellent container plant for sunny situations. The flower umbels are usually a delicate light blue, and appear throughout the summer. There is also a white variety.

Plumbago grows luxuriantly, and can reach 13 ft (4 m) in a short time. But the shoots are rather liable to break, so it's a good idea to site it somewhere out of the wind. It can easily be trained as a pyramid-shaped mini-tree, but its trailing habit means it also looks good in a hanging basket. It is most effective when climbing up a trellis.

Flowering: Summer to autumn.

A leadwort bush with its sky-blue flowers

The flowers of Podranea ricasoliana

Situation: Sunny, sheltered from rain and wind.

Growing medium: Rich in humus and nutrients, very free-draining.

Watering/feeding: Water freely and feed once a week.

Routine care: Tie securely to support; deadhead continually.

Overwintering: Frost-free, cool, light, almost dry; if overwintering dark, cut back hard.

Pests/diseases: Rare.

Special notes: Also suitable for training as a weeping standard.

Species/cultivars: *P. auriculata* (cape leadwort), sky-blue flowers; *P. auriculata* var. *alba*, pure-white flowers.

Podranea ricasoliana
A reliable, undemanding container plant for sunny situations. Its lilac-pink flowers are 2 in (5 cm) long and trumpet-shaped — somewhat reminiscent of the trumpet creeper. They appear in panicles surrounded by very pretty, delicately pinnate foliage.

Flowering: July to late autumn.

Situation: Sunny.

Growing medium: Any nutrient-rich garden soil.

Watering/feeding: Water and feed freely.

Routine care: Vigorous habit; needs a stable support up which to climb.

Overwintering: Cool but frost-free; in light, but can also overwinter dark.

Pests: Aphids.

Special notes: Foliage drops in cool winter quarters; shorten long shoots in autumn.

45

Sesbania

These plants from Argentina have downward-hanging clusters of red flowers similar to laburnum or wisteria (*S. tripetii* is known as the wisteria tree). The foliage is rather like that of mimosa and is shed in winter.

Flowering: Spring to autumn.

Situation: Sunny, warm.

Growing medium: Rich in humus and nutrients; free-draining.

Watering/feeding: Water only in moderation; feed fortnightly until August at the latest.

Routine care: Deadhead regularly to stop fruits forming.

Overwintering: Remove all dead vegetation before bringing the plant indoors; overwinter frost-free, cool, dark and dry.

Sesbania is a relatively uncommon plant.

Diseases: Mildew.

Special notes: Can be trained as a small tree or kept bushy by cutting back annually, the best time for this being after you've brought it back outside.

Species: *S. punicea*, vermilion flowers.

Solanum

This large group of plants belongs to the family Solanaceae, and includes some of the most beautiful and exotic container plants, notably the Costa Rican nightshade (*S. wendlandii*), with its exotic-looking blue-violet flowers. The genus *Solanum* is extremely diverse, with lots of different species and cultivars; the best-known species is the potato (*S. tuberosum*).

Those species and cultivars that are of interest as container plants are very varied in their requirements. But there are two features that are common to all of them — a rapid growth rate and a high susceptibility to certain pests.

Flowering: Spring to autumn, depending on species.

Situation: Sun to semi-shade; sheltered from wind; warm.

Growing medium: Rich in humus and nutrients, very free-draining, not too much lime.

Watering/feeding: Water freely and feed once a week when in full growth.

Overwintering: Frost-free, cool — also dark, as the plants are deciduous. Cut them back before bringing them indoors.

Pests: Aphids, red spider mites.

Special notes: The shoots are rather fragile.

Species/cultivars: *S. jasminoides* (potato vine), white flower clusters, thin shoots, robust, climbs very high; *S. rantonettii* (blue potato bush), blue-violet flowers with yellow stamens (summer to autumn), climbs to 6–7 ft (2 m); *S. crispum* 'Glasnevin', one of the most beautiful cultivars, clusters of blue-violet flowers, luxuriant foliage, deciduous if overwintered cool.

Some species and cultivars of Solanum can form wonderful standard bushes.

A standard-trained cape honey-suckle with clusters of bright-red flowers

Overwintering: Tolerates light frosts, but is best overwintered in a frost-free, very cool and light room — ideally a cool greenhouse.

Pests: Aphids, scale insects, red spider mites.

Special notes: In a conservatory they start flowering as early as April; poisonous!

Species/cultivars: Numerous variants, more or less strongly scented. *T. asiaticum* is more robust than *T. jasminoides* (star jasmine), and tolerates frost down to 14°F (-10°C).

Trachelospermum — these ever-green climbers produce jasmine-like flowers for many weeks.

Cape honeysuckle
Tecoma capensis
The red flowers of the cape honeysuckle stand out nicely against the dark bronze-green pinnate leaves. This plant can be grown as a climber or as a free-standing plant.

Flowering: From high summer until the first frosts.

Situation: Sunny, light.

Growing medium: Rich in humus and nutrients.

Watering/feeding: Water and feed freely when in full growth.

Routine care: To train it as a bush, cut back almost to ground level before bringing in for the winter. To train it as a climber, shorten side-shoots to 2–4 buds.

Overwintering: Frost-free, very cool, almost dry, also dark (as it is deciduous).

Pests: Aphids.

Cultivars: *T. c.* 'Aurea', clusters of brilliant golden tube-shaped flowers.

Trachelospermum
A genus of Asian climbers whose fragrant white flowers are very similar to jasmine (*T. jasminoides* is known as star jasmine). These evergreen woody-stemmed climbers are undemanding plants, ideal for covering pillars or columns.

Flowering: June–August.

Situation: Sun to shade.

Growing medium: Rich in humus and nutrients; free-draining.

Watering/feeding: Water and feed regularly in growing season.

Routine care: Prune as required.

Plants for acid soils

Many tropical or subtropical plants come from very humid regions, either next to large expanses of water (seas or lakes) or on the windward side of mountains. Some of these areas have mild winters (tropical highlands, for example), while in other areas, such as the eastern margins of America and Asia, the winters are cold. But what all these areas have in common is regular precipitation in fairly large quantities and high atmospheric humidity.

The high rainfall means that the soils in these regions tend to be acid and poor in nutrients. The plants that grow there have adapted well to the cloudy conditions: they can manage with poor light, and prefer shade to sunlight. Some have a reputation for being difficult to grow, but if you take note of their particular needs, they should not pose any great problems.

The temperature and humidity can only be modified to a very limited extent, so you will have to pay more attention to the position of the plant and the composition of the soil.

The choice of position can be quickly made. If your balcony or patio faces south or south-west and is fully exposed to the hot afternoon sun, then it is not a suitable site. A better choice would be a northerly or easterly aspect, or a shaded city balcony where sunshine is limited by other buildings. The best sites are those with light shade, such as those sheltered by broad-leaved trees. Humidity levels will also be a factor in your choice. The moister the air, the more sun a plant can tolerate.

If you're growing these lime-sensitive plants in containers, it's easy to provide the soil conditions they need. The most suitable growing medium is an ericaceous compost. DIY mixtures are not a good idea for such sensitive plants. Many of them won't tolerate lime at all, and if the pH exceeds 5.5 they will grow poorly or succumb to diseases. Don't forget this when you water these plants: only use lime-free water (e.g. rain water or very soft tap water).

Azaleas and rhododendrons
Rhododendron
Of all the plants for acid soils, perhaps the most important group are the rhododendrons and azaleas. These plants come originally from east and south-east Asia, with many species and varieties throughout the forests of the East Indies archipelago. Many of them, particularly those from the cooler mountain habitats, have acclimatised well to European conditions. Some can be found growing wild in certain regions of Europe — notably the valleys of Mid and North Wales.

In areas where the soil contains a lot of lime, you can't grow rhododendrons in the open ground, but you can still grow them very well as container plants. Their magnificent spring flowers will make a beautiful display for any patio or balcony.

Flowering: Usually April–June, but varies depending on the species or variety.

Situation: Shade to semi-shade, though some forms will also tolerate sun.

Growing medium: Ericaceous compost.

Azaleas make excellent container plants for a spot in the shade.

Watering/feeding: Keep root ball slightly damp but avoid waterlogging. In April apply a slow-release rhododendron fertiliser, but only a small amount for small-leaved species.

Routine care: If you break off the seed heads before they are fully developed, this will encourage the formation of next year's flowers.

Overwintering: Many species are frost-hardy in open ground, but need good protection when grown in containers to prevent them drying out when the root ball is frozen. In exposed locations it's best to keep them in a very cool, light room during the worst of the cold weather.

Species/cultivars: The species *R. yakushimanum* and *R. repens* are both very suitable and won't grow taller than 4 ft (120 cm).

R. williamsianum has rounded leaves and bell-shaped flowers in delicate pink. *R. impetidum* is a dwarf form, barely growing to more than 20 in (50 cm), with blue-green foliage, and flowers in shades of mauve, violet and lavender-blue.

R. russatum is particularly distinctive. Both the species and its hybrids have purple-blue flowers and beautifully contrasting foliage. For warm, shady situations there is *R.* 'Fragrantissimum', with flowers somewhat reminiscent of lilies.

Azaleas

The azaleas are a particularly distinctive group of rhododendrons. The best container plants among them are the evergreen forms, which are often known as Japanese azaleas. These stem from a mixture of several wild species from which numerous hybrids have arisen.

The azalea hybrids of the *R. obtusum* group are both slow-growing and low-growing, but flower freely and are amazingly hardy. The taller hybrids that derive from *R. kaempferi* are also hardy when grown in containers, but can only overwinter safely out of doors in very mild areas. However, some of the newer hybrids ('Diamant', for example) are pretty robust and can withstand frost.

With regard to their use, the Japanese azaleas lie somewhere between mound-forming plants and small woody shrubs. They grow to 20 in (50 cm) at most, making them very suitable

The crimson bottlebrush grows best in acid soils.

plants for containers. The distinguishing feature of Japanese azaleas is their luxuriant display of flowers in a rich palette of colours, including various shades of red, pink, purple-blue and blue-lilac, as well as orange and white; only yellow is missing. Although azaleas are fairly tolerant of sun, the flowers fade rapidly if exposed to very strong sunlight.

Yellow flowers may be missing from the Japanese azaleas, but there are lots of yellow and orange shades among the deciduous azaleas, whose magnificent autumn colouring provides yet an additional attraction. The deciduous azaleas are further subdivided into five groups, each of which exhibits one special feature. The *R. luteum* group of hybrids contains many robust but very sweet-smelling forms, while the Knap Hill hybrids are distinguished by large flowers.

Crimson bottlebrush
Callistemon citrinus

The bottlebrushes (*Callistemon*) are natives of Australia. A number of them will grow in Britain, but the most popular species by far is the crimson bottlebrush. This is an evergreen shrub up to 10 ft (3 m) tall, with narrow, pointed leaves and red inflorescences. If you rub the leaves, they smell slightly of lemon.

Flowering: Summer.

Situation: Sunny.

Growing medium: Ericaceous compost, or loam mixed with leaf-mould or garden peat.

Watering/feeding: Water freely when in full growth, and also feed once a week.

Overwintering: Frost-free, very cool and light; keep relatively dry, but don't let the root ball dry out.

Pests: Scale insects.

Camellia
Camellia

These shrubs and trees from eastern Asia produce some of the most beautiful flowers of all. If you can persuade a container-grown camellia to flower freely, then you can be really proud of your 'green fingers'.

Flowering: Varies between October and April, depending on the species.

Situation: Semi-shade, sheltered from wind.

Growing medium: Ericaceous compost, very free-draining; camellias hate lime.

Camellia flowers are among the most beautiful in the plant world.

Watering/feeding: Keep root ball slightly moist; don't water with cold water; spray foliage occasionally (but only in cloudy weather); feed very cautiously.

Routine care: Never move the plant suddenly to a different location.

Overwintering: Frost-free, cool and light — ideally in a cool greenhouse.

Pests/diseases: Aphids, chlorosis.

Special notes: Avoid positions exposed to early morning sun.

Species/cultivars: *C. japonica* (common camellia), flowers February–April, numerous hybrids; *C. sasanqua*, flowers October–December, rather less lime-sensitive, tolerates more sun, has a light fragrance.

Dogwood
Cornus

If you have sufficient space for such a plant, the flowering dogwood (*C. florida*) is one of the most magnificent of all woody plants that flourish in the semi-shade. It is much prized for its pink or white flowers (strictly speaking bracts), which are slightly reminiscent of clematis and appear in great abundance in the late spring.

This plant is slow-growing, starting as an elegant shrub that in the course of time develops into a small tree. The leaves are light green, crescent-shaped and strongly veined. Some of the other dogwoods are equally popular for their magnificent autumn colours.

Flowering: Late spring.

Situation: Sun to semi-shade, sheltered.

Growing medium: Rich in humus and nutrients, acid.

The pinky-red flowers of Cornus florida rubra *are particularly attractive because they appear while the branches are still bare of foliage.*

Watering/feeding: Water freely and feed regularly when in full growth.

Overwintering: The flowering dogwood is hardy down to -13°F (-25°C), so can be overwintered outside.

Diseases: Chlorosis.

Special notes: Young shoots vulnerable to late frosts.

Species/subspecies: *C. florida* (flowering dogwood) with white flowers; *C. florida rubra* with pinky-red flowers and dark-crimson autumn colouring; *C. kousa* and *C. kousa chinensis* with white flowers; *C. nuttalii* (mountain dogwood) with cream-coloured flowers in early summer and magnificent autumn colouring.

The flowers of the lantern tree

Lantern tree
Crinodendron hookerianum
In their native habitat, these thoroughly attractive plants grow into shrubs or small trees. Their evergreen leaves are dark green and narrowly lanceolate. The large, lantern-shaped flowers have a lovely carmine shade, and hang attractively from the long leaf axils.

Flowering: Spring to summer.

Situation: Shade.

Growing medium: Rich in humus and nutrients; acid.

Watering/feeding: Keep root ball moist; feed in moderation.

Overwintering: Safe outside down to 14°F (-10°C); in severe winters can be moved indoors.

Pests/diseases: Red spider mites, chlorosis.

Gardenia
Gardenia
Nowadays the gardenia is known mainly as a houseplant, and is considered the most elegant of all the scented plants. In Edwardian times a gardenia could be seen in the buttonhole of every gentleman's dinner jacket. This custom died out long ago, but as a container plant the gardenia is still an ornament for any summer patio.

Gardenias originated in Asia, and reached Europe in the 18th century. People soon began to treasure these somewhat capricious plants, which come in lots of different shapes and sizes. In the gardenia's native habitat there are climbing species as well as thorny ones and hybrids with speckled foliage.

Flowering: Summer.

Situation: Sun to semi-shade, warm.

Growing medium: Rich in humus and nutrients, acid, free-draining.

Watering/feeding: When in full growth, water freely and feed once a week.

Routine care: Spray occasionally with lime-free (i.e. soft) water, but only do this in cloudy weather.

Overwintering: Cool (40–50°F; 5–10°C), light, airy (e.g. cool greenhouse).

Special notes: Gardenias have a strong fragrance, but can only tolerate water that is totally lime-free.

Diseases: Chlorosis.

Species: Very varied, including climbing species. The best-known species is *G. augusta* (syn. *G. grandiflora* syn. *G. jasminoides*), which has large, strong, glossy leaves with pronounced veins, and grows into large bushes that become covered with pure-white flowers.

Gardenia flowers have an enchanting fragrance.

Manuka/New Zealand tea
Leptospermum scoparium

Manukas are enchanting little shrubs that bear red, deep-pink or white flowers in spring. They belong to the same family as the myrtle. They are sensitive to lime, and you must allow for this when growing them in containers.

Flowering: May.

Situation: Sun to semi-shade.

Manukas have small but pretty pink flowers.

The flowers and fruits of the sacred bamboo

Growing medium: Ericaceous compost.

Watering/feeding: Water freely when in full growth with lime-free water; feed every fortnight with rhododendron fertiliser.

Overwintering: Frost-free, cool and light and airy.

Diseases: Rare.

Special notes: The flowers drop if the root ball dries out.

Sacred bamboo
Nandina domestica

If you want something colourful to adorn your patio in autumn, then sacred bamboo is the plant to choose. This delicate shrub is always attractive — all the more so in the autumn, when the white panicles turn into lovely red berries.

Flowering: Summer.

Situation: Sun to semi-shade.

Growing medium: Rich in humus and nutrients, low in lime.

Watering/feeding: Water and feed regularly but moderately.

Overwintering: Frost-hardy down to 14°F (-10°C); indoors, keep cool and light.

Diseases: Rare.

Special notes: Pretty, colourful foliage all year round.

Cultivars: Various cultivars, some of them with red evergreen foliage.

Daisy bush
Olearia

In their native New Zealand, these enchanting plants are commonly known as daisy bushes because of their abundance of white flowers.

Olearia is a very large genus that contains many interesting species. Of these, *O. paniculata* makes a particularly outstanding container plant. In spring and summer its many branches are smothered with a carpet of white flowers.

Flowering: Spring, summer.

Situation: Sunny.

The daisy bush bears a massive carpet of flowers.

The tiny flowers of the sweet box have an intense vanilla fragrance.

Growing medium: Rich in humus and nutrients, very free-draining, slightly acid.

Watering/feeding: Water and feed in moderation.

Overwintering: Frost-free, cool, light, airy.

Diseases: Root rot in wet situations.

Special notes: Suitable for rejuvenation pruning.

Species/cultivars: *O. paniculata* and *O. × macrodontata* 'Major' are the most robust forms. *O. phlogopappa* also has white flowers.

Christmas box, sweet box
Sarcococca

For anyone who enjoys the scent of vanilla, *Sarcococca* is an absolute must. These little shrubs are known as Christmas box because they are similar to box and flower in the middle of winter. Their tiny creamy-white flowers smell strongly of vanilla.

Flowering: Late winter to spring.

Situation: Semi-shade.

Growing medium: Ericaceous compost — acid and rich in humus.

Watering/feeding: Keep the root ball moist, and feed in moderation when in full growth.

Overwintering: Hardy down to 5°F (-15°C), so can usually be overwintered outside.

Diseases: Rare.

Special notes: The tiny flowers give off a very strong scent of vanilla.

Species/varieties: *S. booker-iana* var. *humilis*, strongly branching; *S. ruscifolia*, flowers in March and bears red berries; *S. confusa*, black berries, intense fragrance.

Skimmia
Skimmia

These evergreen plants are grown principally on account of the unusual colour of their fruits. However, skimmias don't grow all that fast, so you'll need to be quite patient with them. The medium-sized leaves are relatively long and dark green with a slight matt sheen. Skimmias look their best when the ivory-coloured flowers are transformed into shiny red berries.

Flowering: Late winter to spring.

Situation: Semi-shade.

Growing medium: Ericaceous compost.

Watering/feeding: Keep the root ball nicely moist, and feed moderately in spring.

Overwintering: Tolerates 5°F (-15°C), so can normally be overwintered outside.

Special notes: Both a male and a female plant are needed to produce berries, although the male plants are sometimes grown just for their flowers.

Diseases: Chlorosis.

Species/cultivars: *S. japonica* 'Rubella' with magnificent crimson buds in winter; *S. j.* 'Fragrans' (male only) less magnificent, but with an outstanding lily-of-the-valley fragrance; *S. j.* 'Ruby Dome' (male only) compact; *S. j.* 'Nymans', particularly beautiful berries; *S. j.* 'Vetchii' (female only) large berries; *S. j.* 'Wakehurst White' (syn. 'Fructo Albo') white berries; *S. × confusa* 'Kew Green', low-growing, widely spreading, with aromatic light-green foliage.

The flowers and berries of the skimmia make it an attractive container plant.

Hydrangea
Hydrangea

Coming originally from the Far East and North America, hydrangeas are among the most magnificent of all flowering shrubs. As container plants they are much admired for their large, often very striking flowers.

Hydrangeas have been grown for centuries in both China and Japan, where they bloomed alongside azaleas and wisterias unknown to the outside world. Not until the 18th century were they brought to Europe by way of France.

The many hydrangea species vary enormously in habit, in the diversity of their foliage, and in the shape of their flowers. There are low-growing shrubs, climbers and larger species that grow into tall bushes. The latter are too big for containers, so it's the shrubs and climbers that are of interest here.

The most popular species, *H. macrophylla*, is subdivided according to the shape of the flower heads. The hortensias have round heads consisting of sterile flowers, while the lacecaps have flat, open heads made up of small fertile flowers surrounded by a garland of larger sterile ones. There's an immense range of hortensia cultivars available in all sorts of different shades, but the lacecaps have only recently been seriously developed.

Flowering: June–August/September.

Situation: Sun to semi-shade; red-flowering cultivars can tolerate more sun.

Growing medium: Rich in humus and nutrients, very moist but not waterlogged; and on the acid side (ideal pH value 4.5–5 for blue cultivars, 6–7.5 for red and pink cultivars).

Watering/feeding: It is vitally important to water the plants generously, and if possible with rain water. When in full growth, the roots must be kept moist at all times. Feed in moderation each fortnight, using a lime-free fertiliser that for blue cultivars must contain iron, aluminium and trace elements.

Overwintering: In warmer areas and near the coast, hydrangeas can overwinter outside if they are well protected. In colder districts, bring them indoors and overwinter them very cool and dark. Blue cultivars are more sensitive, as they are supposed to stand in the shade and so need longer for their wood to ripen fully.

Pests: Red spider mites.

Special notes: Hydrangeas are not so much grown for their shape as for the extraordinary richness of their flower colours — or rather for their ability to change colour. The scale runs from palest pink to dark red,

Hydrangeas make really good container plants.

and from sky blue to turquoise or lilac and purple-blue.

Hydrangea flowers change colour according to the acidity or alkalinity of the soil, and also the iron and aluminium content. To summarise: in an acid soil supplied with aluminium and iron, hydrangeas flower in shades of blue; in a neutral to mildly alkaline (limy or chalky) growing medium, the flowers are pink or red. But of course heredity also plays a large part. Depending on the species on which the hybrid is based, the flowers will either be in a shade of red or tend towards one of those much-prized blue shades:

pH 4.5 — intense blue
pH 5.1 — blue
pH 5.5 — mauve
pH 6.5 — mauvy-pink
pH 6.9 — pink
pH 7.4 — light pink

Specially formulated compounds are available for determining the flower colours of hydrangeas.

Species/cultivars: *H. macrophylla* is the species from which the majority of hortensias and lacecaps are derived. Among the hortensias with their ball-shaped flowers are: 'Hamburg', 'Heinrich Seidel', 'Bouquet Rose', all three pink/red/purple; 'Merveille', pink changing to blue after treatment; 'Générale Vicomtesse de Vibraye', medium-blue; 'Westfalen', deep purple-blue; 'Kluis Superba', dark blue. The lacecaps include some delightful cultivars that change from pink to blue: 'Blue Wave' (syn. 'Mariesii Perfecta'), reddish-blue, vigorous

Blue hydrangeas are especially prized — this is the flower of a lacecap.

habit, for large containers; 'Tricolor', white-variegated foliage, light-pink flowers — plus many newer strains, including some with very strong colours.

H. aspera sargentiana has velvety dark-green foliage and lacecap flowers in lilac-pink; it is very decorative, but vulnerable to late frosts.

H. serrata hybrids are smaller (4 ft; 1.2 m) and variable in appearance. These again are suitable for shady sites. The best-known is 'Bluebird', whose arching flower heads have light-blue flowers in the centre and also round the edge. The lacecap flowers of 'Rosalba' are pink

around the edge and blue in the middle. *H. paniculata* 'Unique' and 'Grandiflora' bear conical white flowers that are especially large in the latter.

H. anomala petiolaris (climbing hydrangea) has large, flat, creamy-white flowers and climbs to a height of 10 ft (3 m) supported by aerial roots.

New on the market are hydrangeas with variegated foliage and lacecap flowers, as well as dwarf hydrangeas that grow to only 20 in (50 cm).

Fuchsia
Fuchsia

Fuchsias come originally from the western Andes. They are still to be found there, high up in the cloud forests at altitudes of up to 10,000 ft (3,000 m) — in a climate that is cooler and drier than that of the tropical forests far below. From South America these plants have spread across the Pacific to New Zealand and Tahiti, and also northward as far as Mexico.

There is a great diversity of species: over 100 are known, some of which are very different from what we usually think of as a fuchsia. In New Zealand, for example, there are species that grow as tall as trees, while others creep along the ground. Climbing fuchsias are also found in the wild. However, all fuchsias are deciduous and send up new shoots each year.

F. magellanica (lady's eardrops) with its many cultivars and hybrids is the hardiest and most robust of all the fuchsias. It grows into a small, loosely upright bush about 6–7 ft (2 m) tall. The leaves are delicate and narrow with pointed tips. The bush becomes covered with flowers, which are long with red tubes and sepals, and violet petals forming the inner corolla; the stamens are red and protruding. The variety *F. m.* var. *molinae*, also known as *F. m.*

Fuchsias today are as popular as they ever were. Make sure to put them in a semi-shaded position.

This fuchsia flower is particularly beautiful.

'Alba', has small white-coloured flowers. As the hardiest of the fuchsias, *F. magellanica* and its varieties can be overwintered in open ground in most areas. The top growth may often freeze and die back, but the plant will send up new shoots again from older wood.

All the other fuchsia species and cultivars are extremely frost-tender and must overwinter in a frost-free room, though there are considerable differences even among the warmth-loving fuchsias. Many species, such as *F. triphylla* and all the winter-flowering varieties, require a minimum temperature of 50°F (10°C). They are ideal plants for a cool conservatory.

In the mountain forests where they live in the wild, fuchsias mostly grow at the base of other shrubs and trees, where they're protected from direct sunlight while still receiving plenty of light and air. The soil should be moist but well drained, and rich in humus but slightly acid.

Sun tolerance varies depending on the species and cultivar, but fuchsias normally do best in a lightly shaded position away from the midday sun. The ideal situation for container-grown fuchsias is facing east or west. The *F. triphylla* hybrids, and also many of the orange-coloured varieties, tolerate rather more sun than do the more sensitive white- and pink-flowered varieties.

Flowering: Summer.

Situation: Sun to semi-shade.

Growing medium: Rich in humus and nutrients, tending towards acid, free-draining.

Watering/feeding: When the plant is in full growth, keep the root ball moist and feed regularly once a week, but always avoid waterlogging as this can be fatal.

Routine care: Deadhead regularly, and tie up standard-trained plants if necessary.

Overwintering: Bring indoors as late as possible; keep frost-free, cool, airy and dark, and water only very sparingly. Overwinter young plants and *F. triphylla* hybrids in light and at 50°F (10°C). Before bringing fuchsias indoors, cut them back by about one-third.

Pests/diseases: Aphids, red spider mites, grey mould (*Botrytis*), fuchsia rust.

Species/cultivars: Numerous species and cultivars, some of which are given above.

Flowering perennials and bulbous plants

Woody plants aren't the only ones suitable for containers. If you don't have a heated greenhouse (or at least a frost-free conservatory or lean-to greenhouse), the larger exotics are quite a problem anyway when it comes to moving them in and out of doors. But that doesn't mean you have to do without attractive tub plants altogether. There's a big enough choice of other plants that will happily overwinter outside — or in a garage if they aren't quite so hardy. Herbaceous perennials are in fact ideal for smaller patios and balconies.

For those who aren't so familiar with the term perennials, they are non-woody plants that send up new growth from the rootstock in the spring. In some cases the growth above ground dies back before the winter. This group includes plants such as lily-of-the-valley, hostas, delphiniums and asters, and also bulb plants such as lilies. Other perennials such as irises, hellebores and erigerons don't die back but retain their foliage throughout the winter.

Most of these plants are completely winter-proof when grown in containers. But for the rather more tender subjects you will need to have a cool, dry room available as winter quarters. In colder areas, even the more robust perennials will be grateful for some winter protection, maybe by wrapping the container and covering it with brushwood or sacking.

There are many criteria you might apply when trying to choose container plants from the enormous range available. One way might be to group the plants according to when they flower. Or you could choose them by colour, or by size. But one thing is always important, and that is to give them good visual presence by framing them with foliage plants. These will emphasise their structure, and if properly selected will harmonise

Herbaceous perennials also thrive in containers — in front a pineapple flower, to the left of it a Canna, *with lilies behind.*

60

nicely with the colour of the flowers. Evergreens can be used for framing purposes, as can bamboos or other grasses; foliage herbaceous perennials are very suitable too.

African lily
Agapanthus

The African lily is possibly the best-known container plant next to angel's trumpet (*Brugmansia*) and oleander. As its common name suggests, *Agapanthus* is a member of the Liliaceae — the lily family.

African lilies come originally from South Africa, where there are very many species and cultivars available. For cultivation as container plants, the main species to choose from are *A. africanus*, *A. campanulatus* and *A. praecox*, together with the many hybrids that have been developed.

African lilies are perennials, and some of them are semi-evergreen while others have leaves only in the summer. The leaves are leathery and strap-shaped, arching outwards. The blue or white flowers appear during the summer, grouped atop long stalks into large hemispherical umbels.

Flowering: Summer.

Situation: Sunny, sheltered.

Growing medium: Rich in nutrients; sandy, loamy and free-draining.

Watering/feeding: Water and feed freely when in full growth, but avoid waterlogging.

African lilies are some of the best-known container plants.

Overwintering: African lilies, particularly *A. campanulatus*, tolerate slight frosts provided the root balls are well protected. However, a better solution for the winter is somewhere frost-free but very cool; it can also be dark (as there's no foliage), but it must be dry.

Diseases: Rare.

Special notes: African lilies must never be allowed to get too warm during the winter, because if the temperature rises above 60°F (15°C) they will not flower the following summer. Don't worry if the root balls become matted. The more matted they are, the better the plants will flower.

Species/cultivars: *A. campanulatus* produces blue umbels of bell-shaped flowers, each about 1 in (2–3 cm) long; *A. campanulatus* var. *albidus* has flowers that are similar but white.

The Headbourne hybrids are the most important group nowadays. They are frost-hardy and produce larger umbels of flowers in various shades of blue: 'Bressingham Blue', dark blue, 28 in (70 cm) tall; 'Delft', lilac-coloured, 40 in (100 cm); 'Diana', blue-violet, only 18 in (45 cm); 'Luly', pale violet, 30 in (75 cm); 'Rosemary', very pale blue, up to 40 in (100 cm).

Silkweed, milkweed
Asclepias
The silkweeds are herbaceous perennials from subtropical and tropical parts of America. They are valued for their distinctive and unusual flowers. A number of different species are commercially available. They vary considerably in their requirements and in their flowering times.

Flowering: Summer.

Situation: Sunny.

Growing medium: Any good garden soil; *A. tuberosa* (butterfly weed) needs dry soil.

Watering/feeding: Water and feed in moderation when in full growth.

Overwintering: Some silkweeds tolerate a few degrees of frost, and if planted out they can overwinter in open ground with protection. Others such as *A. tuberosa* will do much better if kept frost-free in very cool winter quarters. The blood flower (*A. curassavica*) should be overwintered rather warmer, at around 50°F (10°C).

Pests/diseases: Whitefly, fungal diseases.

Species: The swamp milkweed (*A. incarnata*) flowers from June to September on stalks up to 5 ft (1.5 m) tall; the pink to red umbels smell of vanilla. The butterfly weed (*A. tuberosa*) produces orange-yellow umbels between July and September on stalks up to 3 ft (90 cm) long; it requires dry soil.

Canna, Indian shot
Canna
Indian shot (*C. indica*) was introduced to Britain in 1570, but only in recent years has it become widely grown here.

Indian shot and other *Canna* species are rhizomatous perennials from the hot regions of Asia, Africa and America. Their requirements are what you might expect given their origins. If you put them in a warm, sunny spot, they will flower non-stop from June through until the first frosts.

These plants are of interest not only for their unusual flowers, but also for their long, pointed leaves. The flowers consist of

*The blood flower (*Asclepias curassavica*) is a silkweed from the American tropics.*

coloured sepals and petals, and broadened stamens that also look like petals. Their colour palette ranges from pale yellow to red via golden-yellow and various shades of copper. There is a good choice of cultivars, many of which have interesting leaf colours that complement the colour of the flowers.

Flowering: Summer to autumn.

Situation: Sunny.

Growing medium: Loamy, rich in humus, free-draining.

Watering/feeding: When in full growth, water freely and feed once a week.

Overwintering: Cool, frost-free conditions down to about 46°F (8°C); also dark and dry.

Pests/diseases: Snails; rhizome rot if left waterlogged.

Special notes: *Canna* can be induce to flower early in the following way. Bury the rhizomes about 3 in (8 cm) below the surface in a loamy, humus-rich compost. Keep them somewhere warm such as in a greenhouse at around 61°F (16°C). When the shoot tips become visible, stand the plants somewhere light, and when all danger of frost is past, place them them outside in a warm, very sheltered spot.

You can also treat these plants like dahlias and simply plant the rhizomes outside when all danger of frost is past. But if you choose this method, they will flower rather later.

Cultivars of the exotic genus Canna *produce some really beautiful and delicate blooms.*

Species/cultivars: Several species and about 50 cultivars are commercially available nowadays.

The latter are mainly cultivars of *C. × generalis* — these tall-growing plants are among the most magnificent ornamental plants of any to be found, and they also make very attractive container plants.

C. indica 'Purpurea' is a strikingly coloured cultivar of Indian shot, bearing red flowers and purple-green foliage.

C. × generalis 'Assault' has scarlet flowers and purple-green foliage, and *C. × g.* 'Wyoming' bears apricot-coloured flowers accompanied by delicate-crimson foliage. *C. × g.* 'Black Knight' has red flowers and brown foliage, while *C. × g.* 'Lucifer' produces flowers that are mottled yellow and red, contrasting with lush green foliage. *C. × g.* 'King Midas' has yellow flowers and green foliage. Finally, *C. × g.* 'Feuerzauber' (syn. 'Fire Magic') is one of the most beautiful old cultivars, with dark-scarlet flowers and red foliage.

Crinums produce some beautiful flowers.

Crinum
Crinum

Crinums belong to the amaryllis family, and are among the most robust of the tropical bulbous plants. They make ideal container plants for sheltered sites out of doors, where they gradually open their large, lily-like pink or white flowers over a period of weeks in late summer and early autumn. The leaves of these attractive perennials are strap-shaped but elegantly curved.

Crinums don't have any special soil requirements, and will thrive in any well-drained, humus-rich garden soil. They develop best if you leave them undisturbed for several years.

The most suitable forms for use as container plants are the species *C. moorei* and the wide-spread *C. × powellii* cultivars.

Flowering: July–September.

Situation: Sunny, warm and sheltered.

Growing medium: Rich in humus and nutrients, sandy, loamy and free-draining.

Watering/feeding: Water freely but avoid waterlogging; feed once a week while in full growth.

Overwintering: Like dahlias, frost-free, cool, airy and dry; also dark.

Diseases: Bulb rot if allowed to remain waterlogged.

Special notes: Plant the bulbs so that the tips are only lightly covered. The best planting time is spring. Use big containers, as the bulbs quickly expand; don't divide them. Protect the young shoot tips from late frosts. Crinums can be induced into early growth in a warm room.

Species/cultivars: The best for growing as container plants are the *C. × powellii* cultivars. The flowers are trumpet-shaped, lily-like, very large and sometimes nodding, with up to ten individual blooms on a flower stalk up to 40 in (100 cm) tall. The flowers are deep pink, or white in the case of *C. × p.* 'Album'.

Pineapple flower
Eucomis

The pineapple flower from South Africa is so called because of the shape of the flower, which resembles a pineapple fruit in flower. The inflorescence is borne on a long stalk and crowned with a tuft of small green bracts. *Eucomis* species have a long flowering period.

There are only two species that are suitable for growing in containers. They can be differentiated on the basis of their sword-shaped leaves: those of *E. comosa* are light green, while those of *E. bicolor* have red flecks on the underside.

Flowering: Late summer.

Situation: Sunny.

Growing medium: Loamy, rich in humus and nutrients.

Watering/feeding: Water sparingly until the shoots appear, then water normally and feed in moderation until late August.

Routine care: Divide the bulbs every four or five years.

Overwintering: Top growth dies back after flowering; the plant should then be brought into frost-free winter quarters, which can also be dark.

Diseases: Bulb rot if allowed to remain waterlogged.

Species/cultivars: *E. bicolor*, with flower stalks 20 in (50 cm) tall and large flowers (12 in; 30 cm) and large, broad leaves; *E. comosa*, fragrant greeny-white flowers crowned with smaller bracts and light-green foliage speckled red underneath.

Pineapple flowers are so named for their pineapple-like inflorescences.

Garland flower/ginger lily
Hedychium
The garland flower or ginger lily is a little-known perennial from the Himalayas. Its leaves are a little reminiscent of Indian shot, and like *Canna* it requires an open, nutrient-rich soil and plenty of water. The most robust species is the beautiful *H. gard-nerianum*, which easily grows to over 40 in (1 m). Its leaves are oval to lance-shaped and up to 18 in (45 cm) long.

The flowers are very attractive, appearing in late summer. They

The garland flower or ginger lily

are creamy to golden-yellow in colour and very fragrant.

Flowering: Late summer.

Situation: Shade to semi-shade.

Growing medium: Open, rich in humus and nutrients, moist but not waterlogged.

Watering/feeding: Water and feed regularly when in growth.

Overwintering: Absolutely frost-free, airy and dark.

Diseases: Rare.

Special notes: Cut back the flower stalks in autumn.

Species: *H. gardnerianum*, golden-yellow flower spikes up to 20 in (50 cm) tall.

The rare but beautiful Hibiscus militaris

The fragrant white flowers of Hosta plantaginea *appear as late as August.*

Swamp rose mallow
Hibiscus moscheutos

The magnificent flowers of the swamp rose mallow are an eye-catching sight throughout the summer. They measure some 6 in (15 cm) across, and come in various colours from white through to red. The flowers are typical of hibiscus, with their protruding style and stamens.

Like other perennial hibiscus, the swamp rose mallow is an attractive plant that looks really exotic while at the same time it is relatively simple to look after.

Flowering: Summer.

Situation: Warm, sheltered from wind and rain.

Growing medium: Rich in nutrients, loamy, containing silicate.

Watering/feeding: Water freely and feed once a week when in full growth.

Overwintering: Keep dark and almost dry. Leave the old stalks on the plants until the new shoots have grown tall enough to provide protection for later new growth.

Diseases: Rare.

Special notes: Use large containers.

Species/cultivars: As well as the species, there are attractive hybrids with *H. coccineus*. The rare *H. militaris* is also worth seeking out.

Hosta, plantain lily
Hosta

Hostas are classic shade plants with great visual presence. They make very decorative foliage perennials, some of which have very large leaves. Hostas are invaluable container plants for a spot in the shade. Although some of them have very attractive flowers as well, hostas are chiefly grown for their foliage in its many different forms. The leaves come in a large variety of green shades, ranging from light green via blue-green and grey-green to dark green — and there are some hostas with interesting white- or yellow-variegated foliage.

Hostas are long-lived and easy to look after — if you develop a passion for them you will rapidly turn into a collector. Good perennial nurseries offer a large selection — although if you want to grow them in containers, you should choose cultivars that are neither too weak nor too vigorous.

Flowering: Varies between June and September, depending on the species and cultivar.

Situation: Likes semi-shade, but will tolerate sun if kept well watered.

Growing medium: Rich in nutrients and humus; moist but not waterlogged.

Watering/feeding: Water freely and feed moderately when in full growth.

Overwintering: Fully hardy.

Special notes: Late frosts can damage emerging shoots.

Pests: Snails, slugs.

Species/cultivars: There is a wide choice of species and cultivars available, varying enormously in their leaf structure and flower colour. *H.* 'Blue Moon' has blue-green leaves and blue-lilac flowers, and grows to 8 in (20 cm). *H.* 'Hydon Sunset' has yellow foliage and deep-violet flowers. *H. undulata* var. *univittata* has wavy-edged blue-green leaves with a white central area, and bears light-violet flowers in July (height 18 in; 45 cm); *H. fortunei* has wavy-edged green foliage, with lilac-pink flowers in July; it grows quickly to 14 in (35 cm). *H. plantaginea* var. *grandiflora* has green foliage and large white scented flowers in August/September; it is tolerant of full sun.

As container plants, lilies are easy to care for and beautiful to look at.

Lily
Lilium

Lilies include some of the oldest plants in cultivation, and some of the most highly prized.

The Madonna lily (*L. candidum*), a white-flowered native of the Mediterranean area, was for many centuries regarded as a symbol of purity and innocence; it was even honoured by the ancient Minoans of Crete. Lily flowers were seen as symbols of beauty, and appear in stylised form on many works of antiquity — the Romans used them on coins. *L. candidum* became known as the Madonna lily in the Middle Ages because of its association with Christian devotion to the Virgin Mary.

The regal lily (*L. regale*) is just as beautiful although very different. It was discovered early in the 20th century in the western Himalayas, where plant collectors were overwhelmed by the sight of thousands of these fragrant lilies growing wild. Nowhere else has this lily been found growing in the wild.

The genus *Lilium* contains about 100 species native to Asia, North America and Europe, and many hybrids have been bred from them. Among the loveliest are the Asiatic hybrids and the so-called oriental hybrids from

Japan. The trumpet hybrids and Asiatic hybrids are stronger and flower earlier, while the oriental hybrids are renowned for their elegance and fragrance. The oriental hybrids flower from late summer through into autumn.

Flowering: Summer.

Situation: Sunny.

Growing medium: Varies between species, but must always be rich in nutrients and humus and very free-draining. For *L. candidum* it should be chalky, whereas for oriental hybrids it should be slightly acid.

Watering/feeding: When in full growth, water in moderation and feed until foliage turns yellow.

Overwintering: *L. candidum* is frost hardy and can overwinter outside under a layer of mulch. The oriental hybrids should be overwintered somewhere frost-free, cool, dry and dark.

Pests/diseases: Red lily beetle, bulb rot, grey mould (*Botrytis*).

Special notes: *L. candidum* bulbs should be planted barely 2 in (5 cm) deep, whereas those of other lily species should be buried 6–8 in (15–20 cm) deep. When the tips of the shoots become visible, move the plants to somewhere light, airy and sheltered. Always use a deep container.

Species/cultivars: Numerous species and hybrids. For container-grown lilies, try to choose cultivars that aren't too tall or vulnerable to wind damage.

Nerine
Nerine

Nerines are a group of exotic-looking bulbous perennials that come originally from South Africa. There are several species, some of which are hardier than others. The best-known in Britain is *N. bowdenii*. *N. sarniensis* is known as the Guernsey lily because it has become naturalised on Guernsey and grows wild there. Both species have lily-like umbels, each having up to ten individual flowers with very protruding stamens. The flower stalks are around 20 in (50 cm) tall, accompanied by dark-green sword-like leaves.

Flowering: Late summer to autumn.

Situation: Sun to light shade, warm.

Growing medium: Fresh, rich in humus and nutrients, free-draining.

Watering/feeding: When in full growth, water freely and feed in moderation.

Routine care: Repot every four or five years, preferably in August or September. Otherwise leave the bulbs undisturbed and

The enchanting flowers of the nerine

only divide them when they become congested and produce fewer flowers.

Overwintering: Although *N. bowdenii* is regarded as frost-hardy, it's better overwintered frost-free. Choose somewhere cool, light and airy — ideally a cool greenhouse.

Diseases: Bulb rot if left water-logged; grey mould (*Botrytis*).

Special notes: Once the foliage has died back, the bulbs must be kept completely dry. Don't start watering again until you can see the tips of the new flower stalks. It is sometimes two years before they first start to flower. The bulbs of *N. sarniensis* should be planted very shallow; the tips must remain visible above the surface.

Species/cultivars: *N. bowdenii* is the most robust species. It produces bluish-pink flowers in late autumn and should be planted 4 in (10 cm) deep. There are various hybrids of *N. bowdenii*.

The Guernsey lily (*N. sarniensis*) is probably the most beautiful species, and has very large bulbs. Various hybrids are available, with flowers in white, pale pink, and purply-pink with iridescent petals.

Arum lily
Zantedeschia
This plant is noted for its very attractive flowers, which appear in late spring. A tuberous perennial, it has large dark-green leaves and white, yellow, red or pink flowers. These are not

actually flowers as such; the true flowers are tiny and appear on a yellow spadix (central spike) enclosed in a colourful sheath called a spathe, which looks like a flower. The leaves are large, arrow-shaped and slightly wavy around the edges, with stalks that are wrapped round the stems. The plants can grow as tall as 24 in (60 cm) and more.

Flowering: Spring to early summer.

Situation: Sun to semi-shade.

Growing medium: Nutrient-rich, moist.

Watering/feeding: This plant often grows in water, so water it regularly and keep the compost constantly moist.

The well-known arum lily has strange funnel-shaped flowers.

Overwintering: Tolerates several degrees below freezing, but cool, light winter quarters are better.

Pests/diseases: Slugs, which open wounds that then rot.

Special notes: All parts of the plant contain a poisonous juice that can cause skin burns.

Species/cultivars: *Z. aethiopica* 'Crowborough' with white flowers; *Z. elliottiana* (golden arum) with golden-yellow flowers; *Z. rehmanii* (pink arum) with white and red flowers; also hybrids in a range of soft colours.

Broadleaves

Among the hardier trees and shrubs, there are some very attractive plants that will make excellent candidates for growing in tubs and pots. The majority of these woody plants will do best in a spot out in the garden. However, provided you create the right conditions, you can still grow them successfully on balcony or patio without too many problems.

When growing shrubs and trees in containers, the most important thing to remember is

A mahonia surrounded by a host of different dwarf conifers

that they always need a lot of space. Because these plants grow large naturally, the plant tubs you use should be more like bath-tubs in size.

It's also very important to feed, water and mulch these plants regularly, as the root balls must never be allowed to dry out. Also, depending on how much the plant grows, you will need to pot it on once every two or three years.

Provided you stick to the basic care advice given in the relevant plant profile below, there's no reason at all why you shouldn't be able to raise a shrub or tree as a container plant.

Buddleia
Buddleia

The buddleia will be no stranger to garden lovers. Its lovely flower panicles last for ages, and are noted for the way they attract butterflies (*B. davidii* is known as the butterfly bush). The same applies to those species that are less hardy and do better as container plants.

Buddleias come originally from the subtropics, and vary enormously both in their appearance and in the shape of their flowers.

Flowering: Summer.

Situation: Sunny.

Growing medium: Any reasonable garden soil as long as it is free-draining.

Buddleia flowers are both beautiful and long-lasting.

Watering/feeding: Water and feed regularly when in full growth.

Routine care: *B. davidii* should be cut right back almost to ground level in the autumn or spring.

Overwintering: Most common species and cultivars can over-winter out of doors.

Diseases: Rare.

Species/cultivars: *B. davidii* 'Harlequin' is a low-growing shrub with strongly scented crimson flower panicles and interesting cream–yellow-varie-gated foliage. *B. globosa* comes from Chile and flowers as early as June, producing spherical clusters of flowers that smell strongly of honey.

Ceanothus
Ceanothus

This shrub is similarly renowned for the colour of its flowers, which are intensely blue. The genus contains both evergreen and deciduous species, which vary in their requirements and in their flowering time.

The deciduous species flower in late summer and autumn, while the evergreen ones start in the early summer. The flowers appear in many different shades of blue, forming panicles on the young shoots.

The leaves are oval, and blue-green or deep-green in colour depending on cultivar.

Flowering: Evergreen species in early summer; deciduous species late summer to autumn.

Situation: Sunny and warm, and sheltered for the evergreen species.

Growing medium: Open, rich in humus and nutrients — slightly acid.

Routine care: These shrubs may need pruning. In order to restrict the growth of the early-flowering evergreen species, cut back after flowering to just two buds of the previous year's wood. Shorten deciduous species to two buds in spring.

Ceanothus always flowers profusely, but the flowering time varies according to whether it is evergreen or deciduous.

Overwintering: Most of the common species and cultivars are hardy enough to be left out of doors through the winter, although they may need some protection in colder areas. However, if a plant suffers severe frost damage, it can happily be cut back right into the old wood.

Special notes: *Ceanothus* plants don't react well to being transplanted.

Pests/diseases: Scale insects, chlorosis.

Species/cultivars: For details, turn to the table overleaf. In ideal conditions the evergreen species grow into large bushes, but as container plants they are unlikely to reach the size of specimens growing in open ground. The deciduous species are less vigorous in habit, and also less sensitive. There are many hybrids of both kinds.

71

Evergreen *Ceanothus* species

C. dentatus	intense blue	small leaves
C. impressus	dark blue	small leaves
C. thyrsiflorus	medium blue	for sheltered sites
C. t. var. *repens*	medium blue	rather smaller, more robust

Evergreen *Ceanothus* hybrids

'Autumnal Blue'	delicate blue	small umbels, free-flowering, dark-green leaves
'Burkwoodii'	medium blue	
'Delight'	azure blue	large umbels
'Southmead'	brilliant blue	

Deciduous forms, mostly available as hybrids

'Gloire de Versailles'	light blue	large umbels
'Marie Simon'	salmon-pink	brown-red branches
'Perle Rose'	deep pink	small cultivar
'Topaz'	dark sky-blue	compact growth

Clematis
Clematis

There can be few flowers apart from the clematis that have such an attractive range of colours and flower shapes. Because the flowering times vary between cultivars, this means that if you choose them carefully, you can have clematis in flower throughout the whole year.

The only important requirement is to plant your clematis so that the roots are in the shade and the flowering shoots can climb into the sunlight. Provided you can manage this, your clematis will thrive really well even in containers. They need loose, humus-rich, somewhat chalky soil, and must have good drainage. The container should be deep rather than broad, with a minimum diameter of 16 in (40 cm). Clematis need a supporting structure or a host plant to which their shoots can cling tightly. If you plan carefully, you can achieve this in a small space. An evergreen hedge, for example, can function as both a sightscreen and a living support.

Flowering: All year round.

Situation: Sun to semi-shade; root area in the shade.

Growing medium: Rich in nutrients and humus, free-draining, with a little lime and some loam, sand and peat.

Watering/feeding: Water moderately; feed well (but not excessively), stopping in August so that the wood can ripen well.

Routine care: Clematis needs pruning in order to achieve its full glory. The method used depends on the species or cultivar.

Overwintering: Clematis are frost-hardy, but need some winter protection when grown as container plants. Mulch the root ball and put plenty of packing material round the container. Don't water in winter, and protect clematis from snow as it will break under the weight.

Diseases: Mildew, clematis wilt.

Special notes: Plant at least 4 in (10 cm) deep.

'Rouge Cardinal' is one of the most beautiful clematis varieties.

Pruning clematis

Group 1 early-flowering species (*C. alpina, C. macropetala*)	prune straight after flowering to let some light in; remove any dead wood
Group 2 early-flowering hybrids	prune in early spring to a few strong leaf-axil buds; remove any dead wood
Group 3 late-flowering hybrids	cut back in late winter to strong buds 40 in (1 m) or less from the ground

Clematis species/cultivars

Flowering end of April	*C. alpina* 'Columbine', 'Pamela Jackman', 'Ruby', *C. macropetala* 'Markhams Pink'
Flowering May	'Barbara Dibley', 'Bees Jubilee', 'Corona', 'Dawn', 'H. F. Young', 'Miss Bateman'
Flowering end of May/June	'Barbara Jackman', 'Beauty of Worcester', 'Carnaby', 'Countess of Lovelace', 'Daniel Deronda', 'Elsa Späth', 'Kathleen Wheeler', 'Lasurstern', 'Lincoln Star', 'Marie Boisselot', 'Nelly Moser', 'Niobe', 'Richard Pennell', 'The President', 'Vyvyan Pennell'
Flowering July and later	'Comtesse de Bouchaud', 'Hagley Hybrid', 'Perle d'Azur', 'Jackmanii Superba', *C. viticella* hybrids: 'Abundance', 'Etoile Violette', 'Purpurea Plena Elegans', 'Rubra', 'Mme Julia Correvon'

Species/cultivars: Not all species make suitable container plants. The vigorous-growing *C. montana, C. flammula* and *C. orientalis* are out of the question unless kept rigorously under control. Early-flowering species such as *C. alpina* and *C. macropetala* are more suitable, as are the many hybrids that flower throughout the summer.

If possible, avoid waterlogging by not using plastic containers. Ensure good drainage, and put plant containers on flat stones — the water will run off better. In very wet winters, it's best to overwinter clematis frost-free but very cool. Always keep the roots shaded.

Daphne flowers are noted for their wonderful fragrance.

conspicuous yellow-green tubular flowers, which give off a marvellous scent on the first warm evenings of spring.

Another interesting species is *D. odora*, which comes originally from China and bears large clusters of strongly scented crimson flowers in January and February. The cultivar *D. o.* 'Aureomarginata' has yellow-edged leaves, and is rather more robust than the species. There is also a white-flowering cultivar *D. o.* 'Alba'.

Ivy
Hedera

Of all the winter-hardy climbers, perhaps the one most used as a container plant is the common English ivy *(H. helix)*. Ivy is a plant that arouses both passion and scorn, but it is nonetheless one of the most beautiful and varied of climbers.

Ivy is a plant with a long history. Theophrastus, the famous Greek botanist, thought it rated a mention — and that was in about 300 BC. Ivy had its place in mythology too, and was often linked with Dionysus, the god of wine. But it was perhaps more significant as a wedding plant. Wedding couples used to be given stems of ivy as a symbol of love and friendship, or rather inseparability.

Ivy can also be used for various medicinal purposes, notably in the preparation of herbal remedies.

Daphne
Daphne

These wonderfully fragrant plants have been cultivated for centuries. Our native mezereon (*Daphne mezereum*) is rare in the wild, but if you go for a walk in a place where nature has remained undisturbed, you may still find this species in its original habitat.

Even more attractive than the mezereon are the various *Daphne* species that come from other parts of Europe and Asia. All of these plants are frost-hardy, as they come mainly from mountainous regions.

Flowering: Spring.

Situation: Semi-shaded.

Growing medium: Loamy, humus-rich, chalky.

Watering/feeding: Water and feed only in moderation, but don't let the root ball dry out.

Overwintering: Mulch the root ball, and wrap the container up very well in protective covering. If the frosts are severe, it's advisable to move it into cool, light winter quarters.

Special notes: Where possible, don't touch these plants. All *Daphne* species are poisonous.

Species/cultivars: *D. laureola* (spurge laurel) is also a native of Britain, and has leaves that are reminiscent of those of the true laurel. This species has

Flowering: If at all, then in winter.

Situation: Shade to semi-shade.

Growing medium: Humus-rich, free-draining.

Watering/feeding: Keep the root ball moist, but take care to avoid waterlogging; feed only sparingly.

Routine care: You can prune ivy whenever you like, although spring is the best time.

Overwintering: Treatment depends on the species and cultivar, but ivy can overwinter out of doors in most places. In very cold areas, mulch the root ball and cover it with brushwood, wrap up the container well and protect the plant from drying out through frost. Water cautiously if the weather becomes very mild.

Diseases: None.

Special notes: Ivy normally grows in two quite distinct ways. Juvenile growth is characterised by long runners and leaves with 3–5 lobes. Adult growth begins when the plant has reached a certain age, and also a certain height (this change doesn't occur with ground-cover ivies). The lobed leaves give way to entire oval leaves, and the plant now only produces short shoots. But it is the short adult shoots that bear flowers and decorative fruits, so

Ivy can be trimmed into lots of different shapes.

if you don't want to be deprived of these, make sure you buy a young plant that has been produced by means of vegetative propagation from the adult form of the ivy.

Ivy climbs by means of adventitious rootlets, which will cling

to any support. These rootlets are used only for clinging, and don't absorb anything from their support. This means they won't destroy walls. The only walls that might be at risk are ancient, crumbling walls or dry-stone walls (those laid without any mortar) such as are often found in northern areas — and even then they are only damaged if you rip the plants out violently by their shoots. There is no danger whatsoever to sound masonry.

Species/cultivars: There are lots of different species and cultivars of ivy, varying both in their appearance and in their general requirements.

The most robust of all the species is the common English ivy (*H. helix*), which is found in many of our native woodlands and hedgerows. It is completely hardy, and after many years it can begin to look like a tree.

H. helix comes in all sorts of varieties, with leaves in different shapes or in various shades of green, or variegated with white or yellow. Among the more interesting cultivars is *H. h.*

Moutans are among the most beautiful of all garden plants. In this picture the flowers are shown at their best against the fresh-green leaves.

'Baltica'; with its white-veined green leaves, this form is good for very bleak situations. *H. h.* 'Buttercup' has variegated leaves that look yellow-green in the sun but stay light green in the shade. *H. h.* 'Sagittifolia' has very decorative leaves with sharply pointed lobes. *H. h.* 'Parsley Crested' is so named on account of its round, wavy-edged leaves.

Persian ivy (*H. colchica*) also has a number of very interesting cultivars. *H. c.* 'Dentata Variegata' has colourful light-green leaves with grey-green blotches and white edges. *H. c.* 'Sulphur Heart' has really fresh-looking green-and-gold leaves.

Hedera helix cultivars (only a small selection)

'Baltica'	small leaves, green with white veins
'Buttercup'	leaves yellow to yellow-green in the sun, and light green in the shade
'Glacier'	grey-green leaves with silvery flecks and creamy-white edges
'Goldheart' ('Oro di Bogliasco')	green leaves with creamy-yellow centres
'Luzii'	light-yellow leaves with green speckling
'Manda's Crested'	light-green arrow-shaped leaves with wavy edges, turning copper-coloured in autumn
'Parsley Crested' ('Cristata')	round leaves with curly, wavy margins
'Sagittifolia'	very decorative leaves with very sharply pointed lobes

Moutan, tree peony
Paeonia suffruticosa
Moutans are aristocrats among the flowering shrubs. Their giant silky-petalled flowers are among the most beautiful in the plant world. In Chinese gardens they have been grown since the 4th century. In the Far East the peony has always been reckoned the queen of the flowers, and many of our own cultivars come from China or Japan.

Flowering: Spring.

Situation: Sunny to semi-shaded; sheltered from wind and rain; not south-facing.

Growing medium: Rich in humus and nutrients; very free-draining.

Watering/feeding: When in full growth, water well and feed fortnightly.

Routine care: Don't prune, and don't disturb the plants.

Overwintering: Tree peonies can be left outside through the winter, although they may need protection in very cold areas. Protect the young shoots from late frosts.

Diseases: None.

Special notes: If young shoots or flowers become frozen, they should only be allowed to thaw very slowly.

Species/cultivars: There are numerous hybrids in all shades from white to dark red as well as yellow. Two other species of tree peony are *P. delavayi* with blood-red flowers, and *P. lutea* with yellow flowers.

The moutan (*P. suffruticosa*) is a woody, deciduous shrub-like plant, and in an ideal situation it can grow up to 6 ft (1.8 m) tall. Like other tree and perennial peonies, it has very attractive foliage. The leaves are borne on vigorous stalks, and turn a beautiful colour in autumn.

Peony flowers are bowl- or plate-shaped, and may be single, semi-double or double. With some cultivars the edge is lightly ruffled; with others, mostly the single-flowered ones, the stamens are very pronounced. The colour ranges from white via delicate pink to dark red. Recently yellow cultivars have become available too.

Despite the delicate appearance of the flowers, this shrub is very hardy, coming as it does from mountain areas of China. It can cope with temperatures down to -4°F (-20°C).

Don't prune tree peonies. Protect the shoots and buds from late frosts and wind. Make sure the drainage is good, but never allow the root ball to dry out. Provide support in plenty of time, as peony flowers are surprisingly heavy.

Conifers

Anyone who likes evergreen shrubs will find a huge range on offer among the conifers. But be careful: on small balconies, these otherwise beautiful plants can quickly become oppressive, particularly if you have a long box planted with a row of dwarf conifers. Instead, you should try placing a single specimen plant in a tub, or possibly a pair with different heights or textures.

When you choose a plant, make sure you get good advice. And whatever you do, choose dwarf cultivars that won't grow above 6–7 ft (2 m).

Conifers also vary greatly in the colour of their needles, which can range from fresh green in various shades via yellow-tipped to grey and blue. You can trim conifers any way you like, which means you can form them into a nice shape.

Conifers can sometimes look rather severe, but you can soften the effect by combining them with ivy, box, holly or other similar plants.

The best conifers for containers include the low-growing cultivars of the false cypress (*Chamaecyparis*), the common juniper (*Juniperus communis*) and the arbor-vitae (*Thuja*) — and also some dwarf pines.

*This golden cultivar of the American arbor-vitae (*Thuja occidentalis)* would be quite suitable for growing in a container.*

78

False cypress
Chamaecyparis

Situation: Anywhere.

Growing medium: Humus-rich, moist rather than dry, slightly acid.

Watering/feeding: Keep the root ball moist; feed only very occasionally.

Diseases: None.

Species/cultivars: *C. lawsoniana* (Lawson cypress) has many suitable cultivars: 'Ellwoodii', an erect dwarf form, blue needles, slow-growing, height up to 7 ft (2 m); 'Ellwood's Pillar', very dense, dark blue-green needles, 5 ft (1.5 m); 'Barabiti Globe', globose form with fine, slightly overhanging branches, up to 3 ft (1 m); 'Minima Aurea', small, globose form, golden-yellow needles, up to 1 ft (30 cm); 'Minima Glauca', dwarf cypress, round-topped plant with dark-green needles and shell-like branches, up to 3 ft (1 m).

Cultivars of *C. obtusa* (Hinoki cypress) from Japan prefer semi-shade and soil enriched with garden peat: 'Nana Gracilis', one of the best dwarf forms, rich-green foliage, branches turned to form a bowl shape; 'Tetragona Aurea,' golden-yellow needles, height 3–6 ft (1–2 m).

The cultivars of *C. pisifera* (Sawara cypress), also from Japan: 'Nana', globose habit, light-green needles, up to 24 in (60 cm); 'Sungold', golden-yellow needles, turning bronze in winter, up to 32 in (80 cm).

Common juniper
Juniperus communis
The common juniper also has some varieties that are suitable as container plants.

Situation: Anywhere.

Growing medium: Any growing medium that isn't too moist.

Watering/feeding: Water only sparingly but don't let the root ball dry out; feed occasionally.

Cultivars: The dwarf upright cultivars are the best choice for growing in containers. Of these, the dwarf columnar juniper *J. c.* 'Compressa' is the smallest cultivar of all. It has thin, light-green needles, and grows only slowly up to a maximum of just 3 ft (1 m).

Arbor-vitae
Thuja
The arbor-vitae comes in many different shapes and sizes, and some of the smaller cultivars are suitable for planting in a pot.

Situation: Sun to semi-shade.

Growing medium: Fresh, loamy or sandy, and also somewhat moist.

Watering/feeding: Don't let the root ball dry out; apply fertiliser occasionally.

Cultivars: *T. occidentalis* 'Golden Globe' is a globose form of the American arbor-vitae. It has golden-yellow needles that turn brownish in winter, and grows vigorously to a height of 5 ft (1.5 m).

All about containers

As our cities get more and more crowded, so courtyards and balconies are becoming increasingly important. We use them for entertaining or hobbies, or simply for some green space. Then, depending on our taste and the size of our pockets, we furnish them with flowering plants to make them more pleasant. And of course these are mostly container plants.

However, it isn't just the plants that make a difference. There are many other elements that help transform a dreary courtyard or balcony into a space for rest and relaxation. And one of the most important elements is the containers that you use. Besides providing living space for a plant, a container also serves a decorative function.

You can create different moods and styles by choosing plant containers of different shapes and materials. Country cottages are best complemented by containers made of wood or simple clay. Ceramic pots from the Far East would spoil the rustic image of such a dwelling, but would look really good on a city balcony, or on a courtyard patio surrounded by modern architecture. For a Mediterranean-style patio, terracotta containers are the most evocative — hand-made if you can afford it, or otherwise mass-produced. The visual aspect isn't the only consideration: terracotta is also

the ideal material to meet the needs of Mediterranean plants. Aesthetic factors should not be allowed to overrule the practical aspects, although ideally you should be able to meet both criteria at once. The main practical considerations should be the situation, the space available and the function the container has to perform.

On the windward side of a building, or in other places that catch the wind, your containers have to be stable. Beautiful but fragile handmade pottery may prove a very expensive mistake if a sudden gust of wind overturns the plant and destroys the container at the same time (top-heavy plants are particularly vulnerable). Wooden tubs or metal containers are more suitable for such situations.

Clay pots are the classic containers for plants. They look good simply because of what they are made of, regardless of whether they were made by hand or machine. Their practical advantage lies in the characteristics of the clay, which lets water evaporate quickly. This means there is rarely any danger of overwatering, and the root ball is kept at a more even temperature. However, your plants will also dry out more easily. So for plants whose root balls have to be kept moist, it's better to use some other material. Another disadvantage of clay pots is their

weight, which can matter a lot if you have to keep moving them around. Dragging heavy pots in and out of doors complete with their contents can be an extremely labour-intensive task. Another snag is that clay pots are only frost-proof if you keep them completely dry, and if they do freeze there's a definite risk of breakage. The base is often conical or rounded, which makes them less stable. If you

plant one with a top-heavy stan-dard-trained tree, you can virtu-ally guarantee it will tip over. If you can't do without terracotta pots, then always choose them with straight sides rather than with a rounded or conical base.

Wooden containers are rather less vulnerable, but not exactly cheap if you want really good quality. They are ideal for large plants, and if properly looked after they will last a long time.

Good ones are normally made with iron bands around them to strengthen them.

Versailles tubs are wooden boxes that were once used in orangeries and formal gardens. For a long time you could only get them from specialist suppli-ers, but nowadays they seem to be coming back into fashion. They aren't just a pretty shape, because they also suit the pur-pose they were designed for.

They are raised on little feet, which means the base stays dry. They are usually made from squared timber and decorated with an ornamental ball at each corner. They're often painted white, unlike the round wooden tubs made by coopers, which are treated with preservative. You can also get Versailles tubs made of plastic or metal.

Glazed ceramic pots are avail-able in lots of different designs, but these have only a limited application for container plants. The impermeable glaze, and the shortage of drainage holes, can make it all too easy for plants to become waterlogged so that the roots start rotting. But they do make good outer pots, provided that when you water your plants you make sure they aren't standing in a puddle.

There's a growing fashion these days for replicas of those antique containers that can be found in Italian villa gardens. Nowadays they are most likely to have been mass-produced in cement or artificial stone, but they're beautiful for all that, and look very nice in the right place.

Plastic containers are by far the cheapest option, and are no longer just available in black. Manufacturers have increased their range, and make them in every conceivable shape or colour. Plastic containers have the advantage that they're light-er to carry and retain moisture for longer. But this advantage

Terracotta containers in lots of different shapes and sizes

conceals a disadvantage: it's all too easy to overwater plants so they become waterlogged. Other problems include the risk of an unwanted build-up of heat (especially with black pots), and their limited lifespan.

If you're away from home a lot, you can also use containers that are equipped with some form of water storage. There are various designs and systems available that make automatic watering both easy and practicable. They're expensive, but they might be just what you need.

The right compost

At least as important as where you position your plant is the compost you put it in. This must be correctly made up, as the growing medium has many tasks to fulfil. It must serve as the nutrient and water store, it must give the plant something to get its roots into, and it must contain enough oxygen.

The compost must be free of pests. It must also have the right pH level — i.e. its acidity or alkalinity must be correct for the plant that has been placed in it. Some plants, including most of those that come from the Far East, react very badly if the acidity is wrong.

Various growing mediums are commercially available, but the two main categories are the soilless and the soil-based forms.

Soilless growing mediums
These used to consist mainly of peat and sand, but the recent depletion of peat reserves has caused ecological damage, so peat substitutes such as coir are now used. While commercially popular because they're so light, they have little to recommend them. They have a low weight for their volume, and are often low in nutrients. Once they've dried out, they are very difficult to remoisten, as water tends to run off them instead of being absorbed. Also, if you don't apply fertiliser properly, the root ball can very quickly suffer a dangerous build-up of salts.

Soil-based composts
Composts of the John Innes variety are ideal for container

This healthy oleander shows benefits of the right care and attention.

plants because they contain a proportion of loam, which ensures good water retention and the necessary weight. However, any cheap composts offered for sale in supermarkets are to be used with caution. Often their nutrients are quickly exhausted; only regular careful feeding will make up for this.

DIY composts

If you're in a position to mix your own growing medium, then this can be recommended any time, particularly if you can make it up from garden compost and garden soil (pest-free, if possible) with the addition of some peat substitute or bark-based compost.

True garden soil is an extremely valuable constituent. As it is structurally stable, it won't collapse as quickly as garden compost does and will retain the nutrients within it for longer. Depending on the composition of the garden soil, you may need to loosen it by mixing in some sharp sand or grit (available from most garden centres). This will also help to produce good drainage.

Usually these DIY composts contain sufficient nutrients and trace elements, but they may also contain a lot of lime (chalk). For lime-sensitive plants you need to use a neutral or acid compost — i.e. with a medium or low pH. You can measure the pH value of your soil using a simple kit — an average value for DIY composts is around 6 or 7.

Specialist composts

These are composts that are specially prepared for particular groups of plants. The kinds available include ericaceous compost, orchid compost and cactus compost. These mixtures contain exactly measured proportions of the ingredients that the plants require.

Watering

A regular supply of water is vital for container plants. Unlike garden plants, which can also get the moisture they need from rain via the soil, container plants are totally dependent on the person looking after them.

Unfortunately there's no patent recipe for how (and above all how often) you should water your plants. It all depends too much on such varied factors as situation, weather, compost, the container and of course the plant itself. Young plants, or plants that have just come out of their winter quarters, need less water than do fully grown plants at the height of summer. So you have to water your plants individually by hand. It's time-consuming, but it's the most reliable method. In any case, don't allow the root ball to dry out completely — that's just as damaging for plants as being waterlogged.

Watering should be carried out early in the morning or in the evening. If you can't avoid watering when the sun's shining, then you must be particularly careful to avoid wetting the leaves or they will be scorched. When you're watering a plant,

Composts for container plants

Soil-based composts	These are based on garden loam and contain a slow-release fertiliser. The John Innes potting composts have a number indicating the amount of fertiliser that has been added.
Soilless composts	These are made up of peat or peat substitute with sand added for drainage, and they also contain a slow-release fertiliser. Their light weight means that pots can easily be blown over. If the compost dries out, it can be difficult to remoisten. Yet in many cases the peat is too moisture-retentive.
Specialist composts	Composts prepared for specific plants.
Clay granules	One of several growing mediums which act like water reservoirs.

always make sure the whole root ball is properly moistened. If the compost has already become too dry, then if necessary repeat the whole watering procedure several times.

The amount of water your plants need will also vary depending on the temperature. Their requirements will increase towards the height of summer, and also in situations where there is a lot of wind. On hot summer days you may have to water twice a day, whereas towards autumn less water will be needed. Depending on the plant and the ambient temperature, you may need to stop watering completely in the autumn and winter.

Water quality

The majority of container plants are happy with ordinary tap water. Its quality does, however, vary considerably. If your tap water is hard, it will be good for lime-loving Mediterranean plants, but should not be used for lime-sensitive plants such as rhododendrons. Rain water, on the other hand, is quite satisfactory for most plants.

Tap water should preferably be left to stand for a while so that it can warm up to the ambient air temperature. The best system is to install a water butt for gathering rain water. Then not only can you be certain of its softness and purity, but it should also be at the right temperature.

Various fertilisers in granular form

Feeding and fertilisers

Even if you've used top-quality potting compost, you will still need to apply more fertiliser to container plants during the growing season. Especially if you've used ready-mixed composts, the nutrients will soon be exhausted — and besides, a small proportion always gets washed away.

Plants need various chemical elements for their health, for their growth, and last but not least for the production of flowers in abundance.

Some elements such as iron, calcium and magnesium are needed in only limited amounts, while the so-called trace elements — boron, manganese, zinc, copper and molybdenum — are needed in quite minuscule proportions. However, the principal nutrients are needed in much larger quantities. They are nitrogen, phosphorus and potassium. A shortage of any of these usually shows up very rapidly, as does an excess.

All these various substances must be available in the right proportions so that they can be properly utilised by the plants. Magnesium, for instance, which is involved in the formation of chlorophyll, may be unavailable to the plant because the water used for watering was too hard. This will then manifest itself in yellowing leaves. Evergreens such as gardenias and citrus plants react particularly quickly when this happens.

The principal nutrients, nitrogen (N), phosphorus (P) and potassium (K), are needed for quite specific life processes. Nitrogen is needed for growth and leaf formation, while phosphorus promotes good flower and seed formation. Potassium helps to strengthen plant tissue, and also affects the colour and fragrance of the flowers. For container plants it's normal to apply a liquid fertiliser that contains a mixture of all three elements. The proportions in the mixture are given in the sequence N–P–K, and any other substances and trace elements included are also noted in percentages.

Inorganic fertilisers are synthetically prepared fertilisers that contain no organic substances — and often no trace elements either. They come in the form of chemical salts that can be quickly absorbed by the plants. But if you don't apply them properly, they can cause the roots to be scorched. These fertilisers are also quickly washed out of the soil.

The various feeds on the market are also subdivided into quick-acting fertilisers, which produce their effect rapidly, and slow-release ones.

The various **quick-acting fertilisers** can be very effective with fast-growing plants in particular. They are available as a liquid, as granules or in the form of little sticks.

The effects of **slow-release fertilisers** last for several months, because they release their active ingredients to the plants only very slowly. But you have to be careful when applying these to woody plants that need to ripen before they go into their winter quarters.

Ideally, fertilisers should consist of a mixture of organic and inorganic substances, whereby the nutrients are bound up with the organic materials. Many of the specialist fertilisers on the market belong to this group.

These are specially formulated to meet the needs of various kinds of plants. Precise instructions can invariably be found on the packaging.

If you insist on using **organic fertilisers**, then you can use guano, bonemeal, hoof-and-horn or dried blood — and if you've got a garden, well-rotted garden compost. Dried blood is also a very good source of nitrogen, while bonemeal takes care of phosphorus and potassium requirements.

Both organic and inorganic fertilisers can be applied either as granules or as a liquid feed. The liquid forms are more convenient for regular feeding, while the solid forms are much better suited for slow-release applications.

1 Never apply fertiliser to a dry root ball or it will become scorched.
2 Observe the recommended dosage to the letter.
3 Feed young plants very cautiously, and never during the first four weeks.
4 Don't start feeding plants until they've started into growth.
5 Stop feeding in August so the plant tissue can ripen for the winter.
6 With slow-release fertilisers, take note of how long they remain active.
7 Pot plants with matted root balls usually need a lot of nitrogen.

Overwintering

Overwintering plants can never be considered an exact science. The conditions vary so much even within one garden, let alone over the whole country, that it is impossible to give precise instructions that can be guaranteed to bring all plants unscathed through the cold months of the year.

Not only does the weather vary between the different microclimates, and the climate over the country as a whole, but there are of course considerable variations in the severity of individual winters. A run of very mild winters, when many tender plants survive, may be followed by a number of very severe ones that may test even the hardiest of plants.

Unless you have the facilities to overwinter your plants inside, the best choice is to select plants that will safely overwinter outside. There are literally thousands of different species and varieties available within this category.

If you have a greenhouse or conservatory into which you can take the plants once the weather turns cold, then your choice will obviously be vastly increased. In most cases cold glass — i.e. just frost-free — will be sufficient. But if you want to grow some of the more exotic plants, then heated conditions are much to be preferred.

However, it is best if plants can be left in the open air. In warm (or even just frost-free) conditions, plants will come into growth much earlier than they would outside, and this in itself presents problems. They may, for example, grow too quickly, so that they are already too large to be kept inside when the weather outside is still too cold and will kill off the new growth. If they had been kept outside all the time, they would have been still been dormant and the tender shoots would have been protected naturally.

The warmth you provide will also benefit pests and diseases as much as it does your plants. The plants are therefore more disease-prone indoors than out in the open, especially during their more vulnerable dormant months.

Overwintering plants outside

If a plant can be grown and overwintered in the open garden, then it can generally be safely left outside in its container during the winter.

However, there is one big difference between the conditions in the open garden and those in a pot. In the open garden the roots are below the surface, protected from the frosts by a layer of earth. In a container the roots are surrounded by only a limited amount of soil and a thin container, so they are more liable to be frozen solid. This means that if a plant is only of marginal hardiness in the ground, it could well be tender in a pot.

Fortunately there are a number of things you can do to help bring your plants through a winter outside. The first is to place the container in a nicely sheltered spot. Cold winds can

One way of providing insulation is to put one pot inside another and fill the gap with earth or leaves.

quickly freeze the contents of a pot, whereas in a sunny, sheltered position the plant will remain perfectly happy. Walls, especially house walls, can afford considerable protection, particularly in the form of heat. A group of pots will also help to keep each other warm. Even a shrub will act as a windbreak and provide overhead protection from frost.

Avoid placing containers in frost pockets during the winter. If your patio is at the bottom of a garden where cold air collects, then either move the pots somewhere else or try to disperse the cold air. Even a hole in a hedge may be sufficient to enable the cold air to drain away.

In colder areas, or if you wish to overwinter marginally hardy plants outside, you can provide added protection by wrapping insulation around the container. Anything insulating will do — hessian sacking, straw, bubble plastic, polystyrene — although some forms may not look particularly attractive.

It's best only to insulate your pots during times of severe weather. During most British winters they can happily remain open to the weather. Even a couple of degrees of frost should not cause any damage; it is only prolonged freezing that causes trouble.

Another good method, if you have a garden at your disposal, is to dig a hole in the soil and bury the pot up to its rim. The plant can then be treated as a normal denizen of the borders.

But don't leave your pots there too long in the spring, because when growth starts the roots will pop out of the drainage holes and bind the plant fast into the soil.

Most herbaceous plants will retreat below the surface of the compost, and should fare well even in severe weather provided the pot is well protected.

However, where perennials are evergreen, or at least their stems remain above the ground during the winter, then the top growth is vulnerable to frost. Most of them can stand this in normal circumstances, but with many the foliage can be burned or even killed by severe frosts or

A cool, well-lit hallway or stairwell may be a good place for overwintering evergreens.

cold winds. These plants will need to be protected by wrapping some hessian or plastic netting around the pot. Again, you can happily leave these plants unwrapped except when severe weather is likely to damage them.

When the top growth dies, this isn't always a problem. There are some shrubs — fuchsias, for example — that will die back naturally in the winter only to reshoot from the base the following spring.

Insulation materials

Some of the materials mentioned below are commonly used for packing fragile items that need to be sent in the post. Whenever you get a parcel in the post, always look out for any packing materials that may useful for insulating your plants.

Polystyrene sheets

These can be very useful for wrapping up containers and covering root balls (the cold usually enters from above).

Polystyrene granules

These are extremely useful for filling in the gaps between several containers.

Bubble plastic

This is only suitable for protecting the container and the root ball — not the parts of the plant above the ground.

Reed matting

This material can be used for wrapping up deciduous plants, but it's only of limited use for evergreens because it doesn't let enough light through.

Cardboard boxes

Small containers can be placed in a cardboard box, and the gaps between them filled with insulating material (polystyrene, wood wool, cork chippings). To stop the box getting wet, wrap it in frost-resistant plastic sheeting and stand it on blocks.

Garden twine

Some plants — evergreens in particular — may need to be protected from heavy snow, which can cause them to break. If you live in an area where snow can be heavy, then before moving such plants to their winter quarters (which should if possible have a roof), tie the branches together with garden twine. This will also make it easier to wrap them up against cold weather, and they will occupy less space.

Overwintering indoors

Many of the more tender and exotic plants will have to be taken inside or else they will be killed outright. Some that are just marginally tender may simply be moved to an open porch, where a roof overhead should provide sufficient protection. But the majority of such plants will be better served by taking them in under glass.

Always choose the coolest temperature that the plant will endure. If it is too warm, the plant will continue to grow or come into early growth. It may then become a nuisance to look after, especially if it gets too large. A winter of central heating can have quite startling effects on the size of plants by the following spring.

Don't move your plants inside too early — wait until cold weather is expected. Conversely, don't be in too much of a hurry to move them outside again. First wait until all threat of frosts has passed, and then accustom them gradually so that they are thoroughly hardened by the time you put them outside permanently.

A greenhouse is the ideal place to use for overwintering, but a conservatory or an enclosed porch will do. Spare rooms and window sills can be utilised, but make sure the plants don't get too warm and aren't starved of light.

Plants that have retreated below ground, or ones that have been removed from their pots (bulbs, for example), can be stored in a garage or shed — or a in cellar if you're lucky enough to have one. Many can be stored under the benches in a greenhouse.

On the other hand, plants that retain their foliage should be

When you're potting on climbers, you mustn't forget to give them plenty of support.

placed in a light, airy position such as a enclosed porch or a very cool, well-lit stairwell.

When you bring your plants inside, always check them thoroughly, and remove any dead foliage, flower heads or stems. Also check for any pests and diseases, treating for them if necessary.

Feeding is not required during the winter. Watering, on the other hand, is much more critical. Plants that have died back will need none at all until you want to bring them back into growth. The majority of other plants will need very little water during the winter, so you should apply it with great caution and never overwater.

However, conditions can sometimes be deceptive. The temperatures may be freezing outside, but in a greenhouse several days of winter sun can produce very warm conditions so that the soil dries out rapidly, leaving the plant with no moisture at all. Always be aware of this possibility, and check your plants regularly.

Another reason for checking regularly is to make certain that no pests or diseases are taking advantage of the warmth and attacking your plants. Fungal diseases such as moulds and rots can be a problem in a closed atmosphere, so open the windows on warm days, and use a fan if necessary to keep the air circulating. In sheds and cellars, dormant plants may also be vulnerable to attack from mice and other rodents.

There are some tropical plants that flower and remain active throughout the whole year. In summer they can bloom out of doors — in winter indoors. These plants should be given warm conditions so that they can function normally during the winter period. They should be fed and watered as normal, only reducing the quantities if they enter a dormant phase.

Overwintering: a summary

1 Overwintering is never an exact science because:
   - conditions may vary even within a single garden
   - every species or variety has slightly different requirements.

2 Container plants that are hardy in open soil can generally be overwintered out of doors.

3 But insulation is needed:
   - where plants are only marginally hardy
   - in cold situations
   - in severe weather.

4 The more tender or exotic plants need to be overwintered indoors:
   - at the coolest temperature a plant will endure
   - observing the requirements for each species or variety.

Planting and replanting

Planting isn't a simple process. It involves much more than just choosing nice plants, taking them home and putting them in the first containers you might come across.

If you want your patio to look good all summer long, you can't achieve this without careful planning beforehand. The planning process begins with working out how much space you've got available, and ends with the amount of money you have to spend. After all, what's the use of having beautiful container plants if there isn't enough room for them in the first place? And what use can they be if they're too crowded to be seen, let alone grow properly?

Planning

You need to plan your balcony or patio well in advance. The long winter months are the ideal time for studying the gardening catalogues and finding out exactly what you want and where it should go. If you want to choose a particular mood or theme for your patio, then the plants you choose should harmonise with each other.

To avoid disappointments later, think carefully about where you can site the plants. Don't get so carried away that you forget how much space there is available. Container plants can reach quite a considerable size, and you also need to have some space left where you can sit down and admire all your handiwork. By the way, rectangular containers help to save space.

Think about how you're going to get your containers home, particularly if you live in a block of flats without a lift. If you're often away on business, or like going away a lot, don't buy any plants that need a great deal of looking after. And last but not least, take special care if there are likely to be small children or pets around, and try not to buy any plants which could poison, burn or otherwise harm them.

If possible, buy your plants only from specialist suppliers, and make sure they are all healthy; read carefully any care instructions which may accompany them.

Buy suitable containers for young plants, bearing in mind that some container plants can grow really large. Potting on an angel's trumpet in full bloom won't be much of a treat. Also, standard-trained plants will need really stout containers or they will be blown down by the first gust of wind.

This standard marguerite has just been moved to a larger pot.

If you aren't already well set up for gardening, get the necessary equipment in good time: watering can, plant supports, secateurs, wire ties or garden twine, and a protective plastic sheet to work on. And if you're planning to use it, don't forget the slow-release fertiliser!

Preparing to plant

Before you can start on the actual job of planting, there are a few preparations that need to be made first.

New clay containers have to be exposed to water for a few days. Either put them out in the rain, or if the weather's fine soak them in the bath for twelve hours. If you're using old containers, these must be thoroughly cleaned, with hot water if at all possible. Otherwise disease is bound to strike.

If you've decided on a climbing plant, you'll need to get a suitable support for it. You may be intending to attach the support to a wall, or else anchor it in a really stout container as a free-standing framework. But in either case you must do the job before the plant is planted. If you want your climber to grow properly, make sure you use a large enough container.

Standards need a supporting stick, or better still a proprietary plant support; these plant aids are made of metal and available in various forms. Anchor them directly in the container before planting. This in fact applies to any accessories that serve to give a plant a particular shape.

Climbing supports can sometimes be decorative too.

The right time to plant

The best time to plant containers is the spring. This fits in well with the business of buying the plant. You'll have been planning carefully all winter, and waiting eagerly to make the purchase — and now at last you can do so. Also, the range of plants available is normally biggest at this time of year.

The exact time for planting will depend on the type of plant. You may be able to start planting as early as March, but if you're dealing with very tender subjects you must wait for rather warmer weather when there is no more danger of frost. All fully hardy shrubs and trees, or

those which tolerate a few degrees below freezing, can be planted at the beginning of the season. Tropical and subtropical plants, or plants whose young shoots are vulnerable to a late frost (some herbaceous perennials, for example), are better planted later, when there's no risk of frost.

The actual planting

First set out all the equipment you'll need for planting (keeping it within easy reach): plant supports, secateurs, watering can, wire ties or garden twine, protective plastic sheeting to work on, slow-release fertiliser (if you need it), and of course the container and the plant.

Good plant containers have one or more drainage holes so that excess water can drain away properly. To avoid blocking these with the growing medium, put a few crocks over them — broken clay pots come in very handy here.

Next you cover the base of the container with a layer of coarse gravel and a layer of sand — you could also use clay pellets or other drainage materials. This drainage layer should be around 4 in (10 cm) deep. To avoid getting dirt into it, you can cover the drainage layer with horticultural fleece.

You now put some of the growing medium into the pot — how much will depend on the size of the root ball. This is the point where you must decide whether or not to mix in a slow-release fertiliser.

Now move the container to its final location, fix the plant support securely and put the plant in place. Gradually fill the container with compost, pressing it down firmly so that there are no spaces left. Make sure you leave enough space below the rim to allow for watering. Tie the plant to its support, water thoroughly and you will have completed the planting process.

Potting on

However well you feed your plant, the nutrients in the container will eventually become exhausted, and a time will come when the root ball consists of nothing but a tangled mass. If your plant has reached such a stage, then it's time for it to be potted on.

With fast-growing plants such as oleander or *Solanum*, this can happen every year. You also need to give a plant a new pot if the compost has formed a crust and won't take up any more nutrients or water, or if the behaviour of the plant indicates that its container has become too small.

What has already been said about planting applies to a certain extent to replanting as well. The new container should be appropriate to the size of the plant. But under no circumstances should the container be too large, as there are some plants that can't cope with pots that are too big.

Potting up smaller plants isn't too difficult, but with larger specimens you sometimes can't manage without extra equipment and a few more helping hands. Container rollers or stands can help with moving large or heavy containers, and they also make the work easier.

The best time for potting on is in the spring, when the plant is hungry for fresh nutrients. But you shouldn't pot on tender subjects for as long as there's any chance of frost. Repotted plants put on a growth spurt thanks to their fresh supplies of nutrients, which means they are especially vulnerable to damage from a late frost.

A larger plant will be easier to pot on if you first tie it up carefully with twine. Also, if a plant needs cutting back when it comes out of its winter quarters, now is the time to do it — although this only applies to frost-hardy plants.

Now to the potting-on process itself: first loosen the plant and lift it out of its old pot, shaking the old compost off the root ball; if it's tightly matted, trim off the outer edge with a sharp knife. Now transfer the plant to a new container that you've already prepared (not forgetting the drainage layer). Anchor any support, and fill the pot up gradually with the fresh growing medium. Firm the plant down well and water it.

If possible, roll the container to a spot that is sheltered from the wind. This will make it easier for the plant to form new roots, and to survive any check or damage caused by the change of container.

Potting on a large perennial can be a tricky process.

Plan carefully, taking all the conditions into account. Only buy healthy plants. Follow the instructions for their care. Make sure all your containers are clean. Don't forget drainage. Think ahead about supports for your plants, especially climbers. Avoid repotting in cold or frosty weather.

Diseases and pests

This is such an extensive topic that a small book such as this can only hope to provide a summary of the main points.

Container plants are by no means immune from diseases and pests. After all, most of them come from countries with completely different climates from our own. Also, the plants used are often cultivated varieties — the result of intensive breeding — and are therefore generally more at risk than are the wild species.

That doesn't mean, however, that every caterpillar is a reason for panicking — and above all it's no excuse for simply reaching for the chemical cudgel. It may often be enough just to squash the odd aphid with your fingers to prevent an all-out aphid attack.

In their early stages, many diseases can be dealt with by simple, environmentally friendly measures. You can greatly limit pest attack by placing plants next to suitable neighbours (companion planting) and in ideal situations. Various herbal extracts also help to keep plants in good health, either by ridding them of some pest or by not allowing it to get a hold in the first place.

These so-called integrated plant-protection measures should always be the first step, and the use of chemicals should only be the very last resort.

Many of the chemicals used to protect plants have been shown to kill as many beneficial insects as they do pests, while just as many chemical-resistant pests are able to survive.

However, before considering the various diseases and their remedies, there are some useful preventative measures that you can take.

The right plant in the right place

Many diseases and pest attacks are simply due to the fact that a plant is unsuited to the conditions that it is exposed to. This means you can save a lot of trouble by only choosing plants that are suited to the positions

Fungal diseases display a wide range of symptoms.

you can offer them. Plants that like to stand in the sun will do less well in a shady situation than those that like the shade, and will consequently be more vulnerable to disease. Fungal infections in particular can be considerably restricted by the right choice of plants.

Fungal diseases
Fungal infections are responsible for by far the highest proportion of plant diseases. These can occur in all parts of the plant, where they damage the tissue. They appear in various forms, and can often be recognised from external symptoms.

Viral diseases
Diseases caused by viruses can't always be recognised immediately. The most common sign of viral attack is a mosaic-like discoloration of the leaves or a pronounced puckering of the foliage. Viruses normally enter through a wound, where they are mainly transmitted by aphids. But they can also enter from the soil through the action of nematodes. Viral diseases are usually difficult to combat.

Bacterial diseases
Compared with fungal and viral diseases, those caused by bacteria are relatively few. On the other hand, when they do occur they are almost impossible to combat. The bacteria that give rise to the diseases can be transmitted in various ways, both via the soil and from people or animals.

Viral diseases

| Mosaic disease | leaves speckled with yellow, then distorted; growth disorders | no treatment available: destroy the plant |

Bacterial diseases

| Fireblight | shoots look as though they're burnt; leaves die off but remain clinging to withered stems | no cure available: destroy the plant |
| Oleander canker | cankerous growths; plant dies off | remove and destroy shoots |

Diseases caused by pests

Aphids green, grey or black sucking insects which excrete honeydew	puckered leaves; shoot tips die off; plant gets weaker; sooty moulds tend to form	herbal extracts of wormwood; pyrethrum spray; insecticides
Scale insects small sucking insects that sit tight in one place, producing gossamer-like excretions and honeydew	plant gets weaker; distorted shoots	scrape off pests; liquid paraffin; insecticides
Leaf bugs only some are pests	leaves holed and deformed; flowers deformed	pick pests off by hand; insecticides
Red lily beetles brilliant-red leaf beetles on lilies	whole plant damaged from being eaten	pick pests off by hand; insecticides
Leaf miners caterpillars of leaf-mining moths	irregular passages eaten through leaves, which fall prematurely	remove affected leaves
Red spider mites tiny, often red-coloured mites on the underside of leaves	leaves drop as sap is drawn off	difficult to combat: on hot days put plant in shade and shower with lukewarm water; insecticides (but mites quickly become resistant)

Animal pests

The term 'pest' is generally applied to those creatures that feed on cultivated or useful plants. All other creatures are reckoned, roughly speaking, to be beneficial.

However, nature doesn't make such distinctions. Every living creature has an equal right to its place in a properly balanced natural world. When you grow plants in containers, you need to pay particular attention to this balance, for this is the only way to keep these pestilential nuisances in check.

For good environmental reasons you should always start with environmentally friendly methods of dealing with pests. First you need to protect all the various creatures that are beneficial to plants, such as ladybirds, ichneumon flies, hoverflies, bees, birds etc. Secondly, always bear in mind there are many pests that quickly become resistant to pesticides. And last

Whitefly

but not least, remember that pesticides are by definition poisonous. The handling of these substances can damage people as well as the pests they are intended to kill.

Using pesticides

If you have to resort eventually to pesticides, note that they are based on certain active ingredients, all of which are poisonous to both people and animals. They are divided into various classes of poison, which must be marked on the package. Always observe the following precautions:

- Buy the smallest package you can. If you need a large quantity, it's better to use separate remedies to avoid pests becoming resistant.

- Obey the instructions for use precisely.

- Don't keep opened packages: they are dangerous and soon lose their effectiveness. Anything left over should be disposed of carefully.

- Always keep pesticides away from small children and pets.

Damage due to other factors

Besides problems caused by diseases, parasites or animals, plants can also be damaged by physical external influences such as heavy rain, hail or unexpected frosts.

They can also be harmed by internal physiological disorders, of which chlorosis is perhaps the best-known form.

Diseases caused by pests (continued)

Thrips/thunderfly		
tiny black flying insects	white flecks on leaves and flowers	pyrethrum spray, but only if attack is severe
Whitefly		
tiny moth-like insects on underside of leaves, excreting honeydew	damage from sap being drawn off; sooty moulds tend to form	hard to combat: insecticides; sticky insect trap sheets

Fungal diseases

Powdery mildew		
white coating on leaves, flowers, buds and branches	stunted growth; deformed leaves	cut off affected parts; spray with field horsetail broth; fungicides
Grey mould/*Botrytis*		
grey, velvety coating on leaves and flowers	plant rots and wilts; buds fail to open	remove diseased parts; improve ventilation; reduce watering; avoid nitrogen-rich feeds; fungicides
Rust		
little yellow or brown pustules on leaves	leaves fall prematurely; growth weakened	remove leaves (keep away from compost heap); fungicides
Stem/root rot		
rot begins in roots, rhizomes or tubers	plant flowers badly; plant dies off	destroy affected plants; improve soil; fungicides
Sooty moulds		
sticky black sooty coating on leaves	leaves turn yellow and drop prematurely; plant gets weaker	collect and destroy leaves; fungicides

Physiological disorders

Chlorosis		
leaves turn yellow with green veins	growth disorders	water with iron-rich preparations; check pH and perhaps make soil more acid
Sun scorch		
leaves discoloured red, brown or silvery	growth disorders	move plant to a shadier position
Drought		
leaves curl inwards	growth disorders	if root ball dry, water immediately; move somewhere shadier; maybe repot

Index